DATE DUE

JOHN WESLEY'S PRAYERS

Edited by

FREDERICK C. GILL

ABINGDON-COKESBURY PRESS

NEW YORK • NASHVILLE

JOHN WESLEY'S PRAYERS

COPYRIGHT MCMLI
BY PIERCE AND SMITH

Library of Congress Catalog Card Number: 52-5381

SET UP, PRINTED, AND BOUND BY THE PARTHENON PRESS, AT NASHVILLE, TENNESSEE, UNITED STATES OF AMERICA

BV
245
W4

INTRODUCTION

IT is many years since John Wesley's prayers last appeared in print. I have before me the fifth edition of his first collection: *A Collection of Forms of Prayer for Every Day in the Week*. It is paper-backed and bears the publisher's inscription:

BRISTOL, PRINTED:
And sold by J. PALMER, in *Wine-street:* By G. Woodfall, near *Charing-Cross,* LONDON; A. DODD, at the *Peacock* in the *Strand;* J. ROBINSON, *Ludgate-street;* and T. TRYE, near *Grays-Inn,* 1755.

This yellowing copy is nearly two hundred years old, a slim volume of seventy-six pages; but the first edition appeared over twenty years earlier, in 1733, and was Wesley's first publication. He was engaged at the time in teaching at Oxford, having recently been ordained, and had gathered round him in the university from his pupils a religious group, the object of which was the revival of spiritual rule and discipline. It met with surprising success, and out of it came, unforeseen at the time, the Methodist Revival. No other movement is comparable in the history of Western Christendom in its

waves of mounting power and energy touching so many
phases of the nation's life, in the sweep of its world influence, and in the shaping and destiny of the greatest
figure of the English Church.

Maximin Piette, the Franciscan scholar, has paid it
generous tribute: "It must be admitted that [Method-
ism] is the most characteristic movement in the whole
story of Protestantism; the most modern and without
any doubt whatever the most important up to the present year and day of grace." He speaks of its "very
marked importance" in the old and new worlds, of "the
very imposing number of its followers, of the religious,
social, and civilizing activities of its membership," and
of how it came out of an ivy-clad country vicarage and
an Oxford common room.

For that reason therefore and not only as a literary
curiosity Wesley's first publication is important, al-
though for many years it has been overlooked, if not
forgotten. Wesley was thirty years old at the time, and
these earliest prayers reflect his devotional life and
method; also they were prepared and first published
for the use of his university group, so that we may think
of them as once alive and vital on the lips of youth, and
in their phrasing (typically Hanoverian in their refer-
ences to the social hierarchy) learn something of the
needs, aspirations, and spiritual quality of those who
first used them.

"Of his pupils," we are told in Coke and Moore's *Life of Wesley,* published in 1792, "he took the greatest care, accounting himself not only responsible for them to their parents and the community, but to God. He laboured not only to make them scholars but Christians also, and to that end wrote a form of prayers for them (which is still extant) for every day of the week." And Wesley himself records in his *Journal:* "In the same year (1733) I printed (the first time I ventured to print anything) for the use of my pupils, *A Collection of Forms of Prayer;* and in this I spoke explicitly of giving the whole heart and the whole life to God." In its preparation John Clayton, a tutor of Brasenose and an early friend of Wesley, is said to have helped him.

Nine editions followed up to 1755, an indication that these prayers were popular and enjoyed fairly wide use; and also they were included by Wesley in the collected edition of his works in 1772, which shows that he never discarded or outgrew them.

But their main value lies in the light they throw upon Wesley as he stands upon the threshold of his work and five years before his Aldersgate experience, which took place in 1738 and which had profound and permanent effects upon his career. Wesley was already a devoted Christian; the more we know of him, the more clear is the evidence of his strong religious disposition and enthusiasm from his earliest days. Five years before his

full and final acceptance of God's will he was already
aflame with practical enthusiasm; he had organized the
Holy Club (which flourished in a cynical and sophisti-
cated atmosphere) and was busily engaged in his spare
time in a full round of religious activities, including
preaching, sick visiting, and the care of felons, so that
what followed at Aldersgate Street was not so much a
conversion as a confirmation and final acceptance of his
call.

"The first manifestation," he says, speaking of the
Holy Club, "which impressed the critics, was the dis-
ciplined habits of the new society." Its members bound
themselves to regular seasons of prayer; Wesley himself
devoted from five to six o'clock every morning and
evening to this purpose. Regularity in early rising was
a marked characteristic of those Oxford Methodists.
They were scrupulous also in their attendance at the
weekly sacrament. They repeated a collect every day at
stated hours: at nine, twelve, and three o'clock. They
were systematic in self-examination. (Our generation,
we are told, is defective in self-examination.) They devoted fixed hours to Bible study and to works of charity,
and they regarded personal extravagance as a sin.

Such was the background of his first published
volume. The prayers themselves are of unequal quality,
in some cases a mosaic of collects and scriptural phrases
with selections from other books of devotion, including

those of Sphinkes and Hickes, which were popular at the time; but their general level and their entire range and comprehensiveness are excellent. Wesley's own preface makes clear his method, which was to cover in the course of his prayers for a week the whole scheme of Christian duty and doctrine.

His second collection of prayers, *A Collection of Prayers for Families,* published in his collected works, follows the same weekly scheme. It shows that Wesley in middle life retained his sense of devotional order and method, and applied to the family life of Methodism those habits of prayer which had proved so helpful at Oxford.

"Compose our spirits," he says in one of his prayers in this collection, "to a quiet and steady dependence on thy good providence." And in an evening prayer: "And, as we lay ourselves down to sleep, take us into thy gracious protection and settle our spirits in quiet thoughts of thy glory." Again: "Let it ever be the ease and joy of our heart to be under the conduct of thy unerring wisdom." "O meet us with thy heavenly grace that we may be able to come to thee. Stretch forth thy hand and loose the chains wherewith our souls are entangled."

We notice also Wesley's lively and practical sense: "Quicken us, O Lord, in our dullness that we may not

serve thee in a lifeless or listless manner but may abound
in thy work and be fervent in spirit." And always his
habitual use where possible of one-syllable Anglo-Saxon
words: "Lift up our minds above all these little things
below which are apt to distract our thoughts; and keep
them above till our hearts are fully bent to seek thee
every day, in the way wherein Jesus hath gone before
us." Wesley had an unusually clear, firm, and well-knit
style; and these prayers, covering as they do a wide
range, still remain outstanding examples of corporate
devotion.

The third collection is different. It appeared in the
twenty-fifth volume of Wesley's *Christian Library* of
practical divinity (published in fifty volumes in 1750)
under the title *Devotions for Every Day in the Week
and the Great Festivals*, and is an abridgment of John
Austin's *Devotions in the Antient Way of Offices, with
Psalms, Hymns, and Prayers for Every Day of the Week,
and Every Holiday in the Year*. Austin's book formed
the groundwork of a good many eighteenth-century
manuals of devotion, and was revised for Protestant use
by George Hickes, a non-Juror, in which form it was
popularly known as Hickes's *Devotions*. Wesley had a
high opinion of Austin's book, regarding it as appropriate not only for devotion but also for instruction, and

as combining in devotional form a complete system of Christian doctrine.

Wesley, as is generally known, made no bones over the wholesale revision of another man's work, and in the preface to his *Christian Library* confessed frankly: "I have been obliged not only to omit ... but also to add what was needful; either to clear their sense or to correct their mistakes. And in a design of this nature, I apprehend myself to be at full liberty to do so. I therefore take no author for better or worse." His method, though cavalier and, as we can well imagine, not always appreciated, was in principle sound and justifiable; for his main aim was to present from a voluminous mass and in popular form the cream of other people's work. And there is an older precedent: "To use brevity," we read in the Apocrypha, "and avoid much labouring of the work, is to be granted to him that will make an abridgement." (II Macc. 2:31.) I have not hesitated therefore in the present volume to apply rigorously Wesley's own rule. The prayers in their original settings are too long and cumbersome for modern use, sometimes running to several pages; and some sensible abridgment was called for, involving careful selection and in places some small revision or adaptation in the removal of redundancies and archaisms. The prayers themselves have been considerably abbreviated and for

modern use and convenience broken up into shorter
and more appropriate forms.

This third collection is a rich devotional anthology. It
was last published (also in an abbreviated form though
much fuller than here) in 1908, with an introduction
by Canon Charles Bodington of Lichfield, England, in
Methuen's *Library of Devotion*. Also the late Sir Henry
Lunn incorporated extracts from it in his devotional
manual *The Love of Jesus,* published in 1911.

The prayers and meditations in this third collection
deserve to be much more widely known and used, and
in range and quality are comparable with the best devotional classics. The quotations that follow are typical
of their mystical depth and beauty:

O GLORIOUS Jesus, our strength, our joy, and the immortal
life of our souls.

Make me still think of my country above, and there establish my eternal home.

All is unquiet here till we come to thee and repose at last
in the kingdom of peace.

Lord, we beseech thee, forsake us not in the vanishing of
our days.

May our minds never be discomposed with passion.

Rejoice and with your bended knees and hearts adore the
blessed Jesus.

He comes with his hands full of miracles and every
miracle full of mercies.

May thy holy will be all our rule and thy gracious hand our only guide.

One of its finest prayers is:

FIX THOU our steps, O Lord, that we stagger not at the uneven motions of the world, but steadily go on to our glorious home, neither censuring our journey by the weather we meet with, nor turning out of the way for anything that befalls us.

There is a prayer for a calm and balanced mind, beginning: "O God, whose grace it is that mightily rescues our reason from the desperate rebellion of our passions," and a profound meditation on the sorrows of Jesus: "Behold the ragged purple turned into a robe of light." There is also a prayer for pilgrims:

TEACH us, O Lord, to use this transitory life as pilgrims returning to their beloved home;
That we may take what our journey requires and not think of settling in a foreign country.

And one that uses the lively image of a ship:

O GOD, whose eternal providence has embarked our souls in the ship of our bodies, not to expect any port of anchorage on the sea of this world, but to steer directly through it to thy glorious kingdom.

Such is the range and the quality of this unique anthology.

In the three collections in general we see a clear reflection of Wesley's many-sidedness and of the health and balance of his personality. In this connection he had a positive genius for catholicism, or, as we should say today, he had the ecumenical outlook.

We notice too his sanity, his practical sense and outlook; there is something almost hygienic and aseptic in the bracing and refreshing quality of his faith, in its purity and wholesomeness, and in its close association with ethical principle and expression. He avoided sentimentality and was never a victim of woolly theology or cloudy mysticism. He believed in the doctrine of assurance, not only as a theological proposition but as an attitude of mind imparting confidence in every circumstance and activity; and to a stern sense of duty was added a warm spirit, a clear intelligence, and rational conduct.

It is interesting also to notice Wesley's discriminating use of liturgy, holding himself, as he did, at perfect liberty to use or not to use set forms of prayer as occasion demanded; nor can we fail to observe the profound influence upon his mind of the *Book of Common Prayer*. He keeps consistently near to the traditional festivals and offices of the Church, and it is this, along with his transparent sincerity, which raises his prayers above a pedestrian level. As further examples we notice his use of the *Gloria* in the opening prayer of the first collection, and also his Litany of Jesus, "O Jesus, poor and abject," comparable with Pascal's "Mystery of Jesus."

Wesley also published prayers for children, not included here as they follow much the same pattern, but which remind us again of his strong family sense in regard to religion. "My dear child," he wrote in the preface to these children's prayers: "A lover of your soul has here drawn up a few prayers, in order to assist you in that great duty. Be sure that you do not omit, at least morning and evening, to present yourself upon your knees before God. You have mercies to pray for, and blessings to praise God for. But take care that you do not mock God, drawing near with your lips, while your heart is far from him."

As for the preface to his first collection in 1733 it is worth reading aloud to gain its full vigor and rhythm, and read in this way the old words will come to life and we shall feel their relevance, particularly in their emphasis on making God's will our sole principle of action.

Here then is some indication of the devotional spirit which prompted and nourished the Methodist Revival, and of the atmosphere of natural and habitual prayer

in which Wesley and his associates lived and did their
work, and also some explanation of how Wesley was
inwardly sustained during his incessant travels and
laborious activities.

The extracts provided here offer an appropriate anthology for modern use and take us back to Wesley's
sound example in these matters. For Wesley, outstanding in so many ways among the leading figures of our
Western Church, was outstanding too in this: he held
order and method in faith and practice to be of the
essence of the Church. It might be argued that the
material organization of the modern Church is wholly
disproportionate to its true nature and function, but
behind Wesley's organization was a system of devotional faith and practice that would have satisfied the
most exacting of the mystics. Methodists still cherish
their traditional instinct for organization and activity,
but do well to remember that Wesley's spirit of disci-
plined piety and prayer, of regular worship and communion, and close observance of the Christian festivals,
are also an inseparable part of their heritage. And Wesley's name and memory recall us all—members of all
churches—to "a holy spirit of discipline" (Wisdom of
Solomon 1:5).

FREDERICK C. GILL

CONTENTS

The PREFACE to
WESLEY'S FIRST COLLECTION
of PRAYERS

THE intention of the collector of these prayers was, first, to have forms of prayer for every day in the week, each of which contained something of deprecation, petition, thanksgiving, and intercession; secondly, to have such forms for those days which the Christian Church has ever judged peculiarly proper for religious rejoicing, as contained little of deprecation, but were explicit and large in acts of love and thanksgiving; thirdly, to have such for those days, which from the age of the apostles, have been set apart for religious mourning, as contained little of thanksgiving, but were full and express in acts of contrition and humiliation; fourthly, to have intercessions every day for all those whom our own Church directs us to remember in our prayers; and, fifthly, to comprise in the course of petitions for the week the whole scheme of our Christian duty.

Whoever follows the direction of our excellent Church in the interpretation of the Holy Scriptures by keeping close to that sense of them which the Catholic Fathers and ancient bishops have delivered to succeeding generations will easily see that the whole system of Christian duty is reducible to these five heads:

First, the renouncing ourselves. "If any man will come

after me, let him *renounce* himself, . . . and follow me."
(Matt. 16:24.) This implies, first, a thorough conviction that
we are not our own, that we are not the proprietors of ourselves or any thing we enjoy, that we have no right to dispose of our goods, bodies, souls, or any of the actions or
passions of them. Secondly, a solemn resolution to act
suitably to this conviction: not to live to ourselves, not to
pursue our own desires; not to please ourselves, nor to suffer
our own will to be any principle of action to us.

Secondly, such a renunciation of ourselves naturally leads
to the devoting of ourselves to God. As this implies, first,
a thorough conviction that we are God's; that he is the
proprietor of all we are and all we have; and that not only
by right of creation but of purchase; for he died for all,
and therefore "died for all, that they which live should not
hencefore live unto themselves, but unto him that died
for them." Secondly, a solemn resolution to act suitably to
this conviction: to live unto God; to render unto God the
things which are God's, even all we are and all we have; to
glorify him in our bodies and in our spirits with all the
powers and all the strength of each; and to make his will
our sole principle of action.

Thirdly, self-denial is the immediate consequence of
this. For whosoever has determined to live no longer to the
desires of men but to the will of God will soon find that he
cannot be true to his purpose without denying himself and
taking up his cross daily. He will daily feel some desire
which this one principle of action, the will of God, does
not require him to indulge. In this therefore he must either
deny himself or so far deny the faith. He will daily meet
with some means of drawing nearer to God which are un-

pleasing to flesh and blood. In this therefore he must either take up his cross or so far renounce his Master.

Fourthly, by a constant exercise of self-denial the true follower of Christ continually advances in mortification. He is more and more dead to the world and the things of the world, till at length he can say, with that perfect disciple of his Lord, Marquis de Renty, "I desire nothing but God," or with Paul, "I am crucified unto the world; I am dead with Christ; I live not, but Christ liveth in me."

Fifthly, Christ liveth in me. This is the fulfilling of the law, the last stage of Christian holiness; this maketh the man of God perfect. He that being dead to the world is alive to God; the desire of whose soul is unto his name; who has given him his whole heart; who delights in him and in nothing else but what tends to him; who for his sake burns with love to all mankind; who neither thinks, speaks, nor acts but to fulfill his will, is on the last round of the ladder to heaven; grace hath had its full work upon his soul; the next step he takes is into glory.

May the God of glory give unto us who have not already attained this, neither are already perfect, to do this one thing, forgetting those things which are behind and reaching forth unto those things which are before, to press toward the mark for the prize of our high calling in Christ Jesus.

May he so enlighten our eyes that we may reckon all things but loss for the excellency of the knowledge of Christ Jesus our Lord, and so stablish our hearts that we may rejoice to suffer the loss of all things and count them but dung that we may win Christ.

1733   JOHN WESLEY

PERSONAL PRAYERS

FOR EACH DAY of the WEEK

Sunday Morning

ALMIGHTY God, Father of all mercies, I, thy unworthy servant, desire to present myself with all humility before thee to offer my morning sacrifice of love and thanksgiving.

GLORY be to thee, O most adorable Father, who, after thou hadst finished the work of creation, enteredst into thy eternal rest.

Glory be to thee, O holy Jesus, who, having through the eternal Spirit offered thyself a full, perfect, and sufficient sacrifice for the sins of the whole world, didst rise again the third day from the dead and hadst all power given thee both in heaven and on earth.

Glory be to thee, O blessed Spirit, who, proceeding from the Father and the Son, didst come down in fiery tongues on the apostles, on the first day of the week, and

didst enable them to preach the glad tidings of salvation
to a sinful world.

Glory be to thee, O holy undivided Trinity, for jointly
concurring in the great work of our redemption and re-
storing us again to the glorious liberty of the sons of
God.

Glory be to thee, who in compassion to human weakness hast appointed a solemn day for the remembrance
of thy inestimable benefits.

LET the inspiration of the Holy Spirit prevent and assist
me in all the duties of this thy sacred day, that my
wandering thoughts may all be fixed on thee, my
tumultuous affections composed, and my flat and cold
desires quickened into fervent longings and thirstings
after thee.

Let me join in the prayers and praises of thy Church
with ardent and heavenly affection, hear thy Word with
earnest attention and a fixed resolution to obey it. And
when I approach thy altar, pour into my heart humility,
faith, hope, love, and all those holy dispositions which
become the solemn remembrance of a crucified Saviour.

Let me employ this whole day to the ends for which
it was ordained, in works of necessity and mercy, in
prayer, praise, and meditation; and let the words of my
mouth and the meditation of my heart be always acceptable in thy sight.

GIVE thy strength unto thy servant, that thy love may fill my heart and be the motive of all the use I make of my understanding, my affections, my senses, my health, my time, and whatever other talents I have received from thee. Let this, O God, rule my heart without a rival; let it dispose all my thoughts, words, and works; thus only can I fulfill my duty and thy command of loving thee with all my heart, and mind, and soul, and strength.

TAKE thou the full possession of my heart, raise there thy throne, and command there as thou dost in heaven. Being created by thee, let me live to thee. Being created for thee, let me ever act for thy glory. Being redeemed by thee, let me render unto thee what is thine, and let my spirit ever cleave to thee alone.

LET the prayers and sacrifices of thy holy Church offered unto thee this day be graciously accepted. Clothe thy priests with righteousness, and pardon all thy people who are not prepared according to the preparation of the sanctuary. Prosper all those who are sincerely engaged in propagating or promoting thy faith and love [especially ——]. Give thy Son the heathen for his inheritance and the uttermost parts of the earth for his possession that from the rising up of the sun unto the going down of the same thy name may be great among the Gentiles.

Sunday Evening

I MAGNIFY thee for granting me to be born in thy Church and of religious parents; for washing me in thy baptism and instructing me in thy doctrine of truth and holiness; for sustaining me by thy gracious providence and guiding me by thy blessed Spirit; and for so often feeding my soul with thy most precious body and blood, those pledges of love and sure conveyances of strength and comfort. Oh, be gracious unto all of us whom thou hast this day or at any time admitted to thy holy table. Strengthen our hearts in thy ways against all our temptations, and make us more than conquerors in thy love.

DELIVER me, I beseech thee, from all violent passions. Let none of them find a way into my heart, but let me ever possess my soul in meekness. Do thou reign in my breast; let me ever be thy servant and love thee with all my heart.

DELIVER me, O God, from too intense an application to even necessary business. I know the narrowness of my heart and that an eager attention to earthly things leaves it no room for the things of heaven. Teach me to go through all my employments with so truly disengaged a heart that I may still see thee in all things, and that I may never impair that liberty of spirit which is necessary for the love of thee.

DELIVER me, O God, from a slothful mind, from all lukewarmness and all dejection of spirit. I know these cannot but deaden my love to thee; mercifully free my heart from them, and give me a lively, zealous, active, and cheerful spirit, that I may vigorously perform whatever thou commandest and be ever ardent to obey in all things thy holy love.

DELIVER me, O God, from all idolatrous love of any creature. Preserve me from all such blind affection. Be thou a guard to all my desires. And be thou my security, that I may never open my heart to anything but out of love to Thee.

ABOVE all, deliver me from all idolatrous self-love. My choice and desire is to love myself, as all other creatures, in and for thee. Oh, let thy almighty arm so stablish, strengthen, and settle me that thou mayest ever be the ground and pillar of all my love.

LET thy glorious name be duly honored and loved by all the creatures which thou hast made. Let thy infinite goodness and greatness be ever adored by angels and men. May thy Church be protected from all the powers of darkness. Vouchsafe to all who call themselves by thy name one short glimpse of thy goodness. Send forth thy blessed Spirit into the midst of these sinful nations, and make us a holy people. Stir up the heart of our Sovereign and of all whom thou hast set over us, that they may be happy instruments in thy hand of promoting this good work.

THOU Shepherd of Israel, vouchsafe to receive me this night and ever into thy protection. Accept my poor services, and pardon the sinfulness of these and all my holy duties. Let it be thy good pleasure to put a period to sin and misery, to infirmity and death, and to hasten thy Kingdom; that we, with all that wait for thy salvation, may eternally love and praise thee, O God the Father, God the Son, and God the Holy Ghost, throughout all ages, world without end.

Monday Morning

BLESSED be thy love for giving thy Son to die for our sins, for the means of grace, and for the hope of glory.

Blessed be thy love for all the temporal benefits which thou hast with a liberal hand poured out upon me; for my health and strength, food and raiment, and all other necessities with which thou hast provided thy sinful servant.

I also bless thee that after all my refusals of thy grace thou still hast patience with me, hast preserved me this night and given me yet another day to renew and perfect my repentance.

PARDON, good Lord, all my former sins, and make me every day more zealous and diligent to improve every opportunity of building up my soul in thy faith, love, and obedience.

Make thyself always present to my mind, and let thy love fill and rule my soul in all those places, companies, and employments to which thou callest me this day.

In all my passage through this world suffer not my heart to be set upon it, but always fix my single eye and my undivided affections on the prize of my high calling.

This one thing let me do: let me so press toward this as to make all things else minister unto it, and be careful so to use them as thereby to fit my soul for that pure bliss which thou hast prepared for those that love thee.

O THOU who art good and doest good, who extendest thy lovingkindness to all mankind, the work of thine hands, thine image, capable of knowing and loving thee eternally; suffer me to exclude none, O Lord, from my charity who are the objects of thy mercy, but let me treat all my neighbors with that tender care which is due to thy servants and to thy children.

LET no temptation expose me to ingratitude or make me forfeit thy lovingkindness, which is better than life itself; but grant that I may assist all my brethren with my prayers where I cannot reach them with actual services. Make me zealous to embrace all occasions that may minister to their happiness. Let thy love to me be the pattern of my love to them.

EXTEND thy mercy to all men and let them become thy faithful servants. Let all Christians live up to the holy religion which they profess. Be entreated for us, good Lord. Be glorified by our reformation and not by our destruction. Be favorable to thy people. Give us grace to put a period to our provocations. Defend our Church from schism, heresy, and sacrilege, and the King from all treasons and conspiracies. Bless the clergy with apostolical graces, exemplary lives, and sound doctrine. Grant to the Cabinet wisdom from above, to all magistrates integrity and zeal, to the universities quietness and industry, and to the Lords and Commons pious, peaceable, and loyal hearts.

PRESERVE my parents, friends and relations, and all mankind in their souls and bodies. Forgive mine enemies, and in thy due time make them kindly affectioned toward me. Have mercy on all who are afflicted in mind, body, or estate. Give them patience under their sufferings and a happy issue out of all their afflictions. And grant that we, with those who are already dead in thy faith and fear, may together partake of a joyful resurrection through him who liveth and reigneth with thee and the Holy Ghost, one God, world without end.

Monday Evening

MOST great and glorious Lord God, I desire to prostrate myself before thy divine majesty, under a deep sense of my unworthiness, and with sorrow, shame, and confusion of face to confess I have by my manifold transgressions deserved thy severest visitations. Father, I have sinned against heaven and am no more worthy to be called thy son. For Jesus Christ, his sake, graciously receive me. Accept my imperfect repentance and send thy spirit of adoption into my heart, that I may again be owned by thee, call thee Father, and share in the blessings of thy children.

Adored be thy goodness for all the benefits thou hast already from time to time bestowed on me, for the good things of this life and the hope of eternal happiness. Particularly I offer to thee my humblest thanks for thy preservation of me this day. If I have escaped any sin, it is the effect of thy restraining grace. If I have avoided any danger, it was thy hand directed me. To thy holy name be ascribed the honor and glory. Oh, let the sense of all thy blessings have this effect upon me—to make me daily more diligent in devoting myself, all I am, and all I have to thy glory.

O God, fill my soul with so entire a love of thee that I may love nothing but for thy sake and in subordination to thy love. Give me grace to study thy knowledge daily, that the more I know thee, the more I may love thee. Create in me a zealous obedience to all thy commands, a cheerful patience under all thy chastisements, and a thankful resignation to all thy disposals. Let it be the one business of my life to glorify thee, by every word of my tongue, by every work of my hand·

by professing thy truth, and by engaging all men, so far as in me lies, to glorify and love thee.

LET thy unwearied and tender love to me make my love unwearied and tender to my neighbor, zealous to pray for and to procure and promote his health and safety, ease and happiness; and active to comfort, succor, and relieve all whom thy love and their own necessities recommend to my charity. Make me peaceable and reconcilable, easy to forgive, and glad to return good for evil. Make me like thyself, all kindness and benignity, all goodness and gentleness, all meekness and long-suffering. And, O thou Lover of souls, raise in me a compassionate zeal to save the life, the eternal life, of souls, and to reclaim the wicked and win them to thy love.

BE pleased, O Lord, to take me, with my parents, my friends and relations, and my enemies, into thy almighty protection this night. Refresh me with such comfortable rest that I may rise more fit for thy service. Let me lie down with holy thoughts of thee, and when I wake, let me be still present with thee.

SHOW mercy to the whole world, O Father of all. Let the gospel of thy Son run and be glorified throughout all the earth. Let it be made known to all infidels and

obeyed by all Christians. Be merciful to this Church and
nation. Give unto those responsible a discerning spirit
that they may make choice of fit persons to serve in thy
sacred ministry; and enable all who are ordained to
any holy function diligently to feed the flocks committed to their charge, instructing them in saving
knowledge, guiding them by their example, praying for
and blessing them, exercising spiritual discipline in thy
Church, and duly administering thy holy sacraments.

MULTIPLY thy blessings on our Sovereign, on the royal
family, and on the Lords and Commons of this land;
that they may all, according to the several talents they
have received, be faithful instruments of thy glory.

Tuesday Morning

ETERNAL and merciful Father, I give thee humble
thanks (increase my thankfulness, I beseech thee) for
all the blessings, spiritual and temporal, which in the
riches of thy mercy, thou hast poured down upon me.

MAY all my thoughts, words, and works tend to thy
glory. Heal, O Father of mercies, all my infirmities

strengthen me against all my follies, and forgive me all my sins.

LET me learn of thee to be meek and lowly. Pour into me the whole spirit of humility. Fill, I beseech thee, every part of my soul with it, and make it the constant, ruling habit of my mind, that all my other tempers may arise from it; that I may have no thoughts, no desires, no designs, but such as are the true fruit of a lowly spirit.

BLESS, O gracious Father, all the nations whom thou hast placed upon the earth, with the knowledge of thee, the only true God; but especially bless thy holy catholic Church and fill it with truth and grace. Where it is corrupt, purge it; where it is in error, rectify it; where it is right, confirm it; where it is divided and rent asunder, heal the breaches thereof. Replenish all whom thou hast called to any office therein with truth of doctrine and innocency of life. Let their prayers be as precious incense in thy sight, that their cries and tears for the City of God may not be in vain.

HAVE mercy upon this kingdom and forgive the sins of this people. Turn thee unto us, bless us, and cause thy face to shine on our desolations.

Tuesday Evening

HAVE mercy upon me, O God, after thy great goodness; and after the multitude of thy mercies do away mine offenses. Let thy unspeakable mercy free me from the sins I have committed and deliver me from the punishment I have deserved. Oh, save me from every work of darkness and cleanse me from all filthiness of flesh and spirit, that for the time to come I may with a pure heart and mind follow thee, the only true God.

O LAMB of God, who both by thy example and precept didst instruct us to be meek and humble; give me grace throughout my whole life in every thought, word, and work to imitate thy meekness and humility. Mortify in me the whole body of pride.

GRANT, O Lord, that I may look for nothing, claim nothing, and resent nothing; that I may go through all the scenes of life, not seeking my own glory, but looking wholly unto thee and acting wholly for thee.

O THOU Giver of every good and perfect gift, if at any time thou pleasest to work by my hand, teach me to discern what is my own from what is another's and to render unto thee the things that are thine. As all the

good that is done on earth, thou doest it thyself, let
me ever return to thee all the glory. Let me as a pure
crystal transmit all the light thou pourest upon me.

MAKE me to remember thee on my bed and think upon
thee when I am waking. Thou hast preserved me from
all the dangers of the day past. Under the shadow of
thy wings let me pass this night in comfort and peace.

Wednesday Morning

O THOU who dwellest in the light which no man can
approach, in whose presence there is no night, in the
light of whose countenance there is perpetual day; I,
thy sinful servant, whom thou hast preserved this night,
who live by thy power this day, bless and glorify thee
for the defense of thy almighty providence, and
humbly pray thee that this and all my days may be
wholly devoted to thy service. Send thy Holy Spirit
to be the guide of all my ways and the sanctifier of my
soul and body. Save, defend, and build me up in thy
fear and love. Give unto me the light of thy countenance, peace from heaven, and the salvation of my soul
in the day of the Lord Jesus.

O Thou who art the way, the truth, and the life, thou hast said no man can follow thee unless he renounce himself. Thou hast laid nothing upon us but what the design of thy love made necessary for us. May I ever renounce my own and do thy blessed will in all things.

O Thou whose whole life did cry aloud, "Father, not mine, but thy will be done"; give me grace to walk after thy pattern, to tread in thy steps.

Strengthen my soul that I may be temperate in all things, that I may never use any of thy creatures but in order to some end thou commandest me to pursue and in that measure and manner which most conduces to it. Let me never gratify any desire which has not thee for its ultimate object. Let me ever abstain from all pleasures which do not prepare me for taking pleasure in thee, as knowing that all such war against the soul and tend to alienate it from thee. Save me from ever indulging either the desire of the flesh, the desire of the eye, or the pride of life. Set a watch, O Lord, over my senses and appetites, my passions and understanding, that I may resolutely deny them every gratification which has no tendency to thy glory. Oh, train me up in this good way that, when I am old, I may not depart from it.

HEAR also my prayers for all mankind, and guide their feet into the way of peace; for thy holy Church, let her live by thy Spirit and reign in thy glory. Remember that branch of it which thou hast planted in these kingdoms, especially the stewards of thy holy mysteries; give them such zeal, diligence, and wisdom that they may save both themselves and those that hear them.

LET these my prayers, O Lord, find access to the throne of grace, through the Son of thy love, Jesus Christ the righteous; to whom, with thee, O Father, in the unity of the Spirit, be all love and obedience, now and forever.

Wednesday Evening

O LORD, my judge, thou art also my redeemer.

I have sinned, but thou, O blessed Jesus, art my advocate.

Gracious Lord, spare thy servant whom thou hast redeemed with thy most precious blood.

Deliver me from the power of sin and preserve me from the punishment of it.

THOU whose mercy is without measure, whose goodness is unspeakable; despise not thy returning servant who earnestly begs for pardon and reconciliation. Grant me the forgiveness of what is past and a perfect repentance of all my sins, that for the time to come I may with a pure spirit do thy will, O God, walking humbly with thee, conversing charitably with all men, possessing my soul in resignation and holiness, and my body in sanctification and honor.

THOU great Shepherd of souls, bring home into thy fold all that are gone astray. Preserve thy Church from all heresy and schism, from all that persecute or oppose the truth; and give unto thy ministers wisdom and holiness and the powerful aid of thy blessed Spirit.

ADVANCE the just interests and preserve the persons of all Christian princes, especially our Sovereign. Give to him and his royal family, and to all his subjects in their several stations, particularly those that are in authority among them, grace to do thy will in this world and eternal glory in the world to come.

BLESS, O Lord, all our nurseries of piety and schools of learning, that they may devote all their studies to thy glory. Have mercy on all that are in affliction. Remember the poor and needy, the widow and fatherless, the friendless and oppressed. Heal the sick and languishing, and when thou seest it expedient for them, receive them into thine everlasting kingdom.

I praise thee for thy continual preservation of me, for thy fatherly protection over me this day, for all the comforts with which thou hast surrounded me, spiritual and temporal, particularly for leave now to pray unto thee. Accept my poor services; pardon the sinfulness of this and all my holy duties; and bless me, my friends and relations, my benefactors and enemies, this night and forever, with the blessings of thy children.

These my prayers, O most merciful Father, vouchsafe to hear through the mediation of Jesus Christ, our redeemer, who with thee and the Holy Ghost is worshiped and glorified in all churches of the saints, one God, blessed forever.

Thursday Morning

Eternal God, my sovereign Lord, I acknowledge all I am, all I have, is thine. Give me such a sense of thy infinite goodness that I may return to thee all possible love and obedience.

I HUMBLY and heartily thank thee for all the favors thou
hast bestowed on me: for creating me after thine own
image, for daily preserving me by thy good providence,
for redeeming me by the death of thy blessed Son, and
for the assistance of thy Holy Spirit; for causing me to
be born in a Christian country, for blessing me with
plentiful means of salvation, with religious parents and
friends, and frequent returns of thy ever blessed sacrament. I also thank thee for thy temporal blessings; for
the preservation of me this night, for my health,
strength, food, raiment, and all the other comforts and
necessities of life.

AND, O Father of mercies, I most humbly implore
forgiveness of all my sins. Lo, I come now to do thy
will alone and am resolved by thy assistance to have
no longer any choice of my own, but with singleness of
heart to obey thy good pleasure. Father, not my will
but thine be done in all my thoughts, words, and actions.

O THOU all-sufficient God of angels and men, who art
above all, and through all, and in all; from whom, by
whom, and in whom are all things; in whom we live
and move and have our being—may my will be as en-

tirely and continually derived from thine as my being and happiness are.

O SOVEREIGN GOODNESS, O mighty Wisdom, thou dost order and govern all things, even the most minute, even the most noxious, to thy glory and the good of those that love thee. O Father of the families of heaven and earth, thou so disposest all events as may best magnify thy goodness to all thy children, especially those whose eyes wait upon thee. I most humbly beseech thee, teach me to adore all thy ways though I cannot comprehend them. Teach me to be glad that thou art King and to give thee thanks for all things that befall me. And for that which is to come give me thy grace to do in all things what pleaseth thee, and then with an absolute submission to thy wisdom to leave the issues of them in thy hand.

HELP me with thy grace that whatsoever I shall do or suffer this day may tend to thy glory. Keep me in love to thee and to all men. Do thou direct my paths and teach me to set thee always before me. Let not the things of this life, or my manifold concerns therein, alienate any part of my affections from thee, nor let me ever pursue or regard them but for thee and in obedience to thy will.

EXTEND, O Lord, thy pity to the whole race of mankind. Enlighten the Gentiles with thy truth and bring into thy flock thy ancient people the Jews. Be gracious to thy Church and grant that she may always preserve that doctrine and discipline which thou hast delivered to her. Grant that all of this nation may, whatsoever they do, do all to thy glory. Bless all nurses of true religion and useful learning and let them not neglect the end of their institution. Be merciful to all that are in distress, that struggle with pain, poverty, or reproach. Be thou a guide to them that travel by land or water. Give a strong and quiet spirit to those who are condemned to death, liberty to prisoners and captives, and ease and cheerfulness to every sad heart. Give to all in error the light of thy truth. Bring all sinners to repentance. And give to all heretics humility and grace to make amends to thy Church by the public acknowledgment of a holy faith.

Thursday Evening

MY LORD and my God, thou seest my heart, and my desires are not hid from thee.

I am ashamed when I think how long I have lived a stranger to thee.

Lord, hear me, help me, and show mercy unto me, for Jesus Christ's sake.

To thee, O God, Father, Son, and Holy Ghost, Creator, Redeemer, and Sanctifier, I give up myself entirely; may I no longer serve myself, but thee, all the days of my life.

I GIVE thee my understanding; may it be my only care to know thee, thy perfections, thy works, and thy will.

I give thee my will. Whatsoever thou willest, may I will and that only. May I will thy glory in all things.

I give thee my affections. Do thou dispose of them all. Be thou my love, my fear, my joy. And may nothing have any share in them but with respect to thee and for thy sake. What thou lovest may I love; what thou hatest may I hate; and that in such measure as thou art pleased to prescribe me.

I give thee my body. May I glorify thee with it and preserve it holy, fit for thee, O God, to dwell in. May I neither indulge it nor use too much rigor toward it, but keep it, as far as in me lies, healthy, vigorous, and active, and fit to do thee all manner of service which thou shalt call for.

I give thee all my worldly goods. May I prize them and use them only for thee. May I faithfully restore to thee in thy poor all thou hast entrusted me with above the necessities of my life and be content to part with them too whenever thou shalt require them at my hands.

I give thee my credit and reputation. May I never value them but only in respect of thee, nor endeavor to maintain them but as they may do thee service and advance thy honor in the world.

I give thee myself and my all. Let me look upon myself to be nothing and to have nothing out of thee. Be thou the sole disposer and governor of myself and all I have. Be thou my portion and my all.

O God, when hereafter I shall be tempted to break this solemn engagement, when I shall be pressed to conform to the world and to the company and customs that surround me, may my answer be: I am not my own. I am not for myself, nor for the world, but for my God. I will give unto God the things which are God's. God be merciful to me a sinner.

HAVE mercy, O Father of the spirits of all flesh, on all mankind. Convert all men to thy truth. Bless the Church; heal its branches and establish it in truth and peace. Preserve and defend all Christian princes, especially our Sovereign and his family. Be merciful to this nation. Bless the clergy with soundness of doctrine and purity of life, the government with wisdom, the magistrates with integrity and zeal, and the people with loyalty. Bless the universities with learning and holiness, that they may afford a constant supply of men to do thee service.

SHOWER down thy graces on all my relations, on all my friends and all that belong to this family. Comfort and relieve those that labor under any difficulties of body or mind, especially those who suffer for the testimony of a good conscience. And grant us all, together with thy whole Church, an entrance into thine everlasting Kingdom, through Jesus Christ, to whom with thee and the blessed Spirit, three persons and one God, be ascribed all majesty, dominion, and power, now and forevermore.

Friday Morning

MERCIFULLY this day watch over me with the eyes of thy mercy. Direct my soul and body according to the rule of thy will, and fill my heart with thy Holy Spirit, that I may pass this day and all the rest of my days to thy glory.

O SAVIOUR of the world, God of God, Light of Light, thou that art the brightness of thy Father's glory, the express image of his person, thou that hast destroyed the power of the devil, that hast overcome death, that sitteth at the right hand of the Father, thou that wilt speedily come down in thy Father's glory to judge all men according to their works; be thou my light and my peace. Destroy the power of the devil in me and make me a new creature.

O THOU who didst cast seven devils out of Mary Magdalene, cast out of my heart all corrupt affections.

O Thou who didst raise Lazarus from the dead, raise me from the death of sin.

Thou who didst cleanse the lepers, heal the sick, and give sight to the blind, heal the diseases of my soul, open my eyes and fix them singly on the prize of my high calling, and cleanse my heart from every desire but that of advancing thy glory.

O Jesus, poor and abject, unknown and despised, have mercy upon me and let me not be ashamed to follow thee.

O Jesus, hated, calumniated, and persecuted, have mercy upon me and let me not be afraid to come after thee.

O Jesus, betrayed and sold at a vile price, have mercy upon me and make me content to be as my Master.

O Jesus, blasphemed, accused, and wrongfully condemned, have mercy upon me and teach me to endure the contradiction of sinners.

O Jesus, clothed with a habit of reproach and shame, have mercy upon me and let me not seek my own glory.

O Jesus, insulted, mocked, and spit upon, have mercy upon me and let me run with patience the race set before me.

O Jesus, dragged to the pillar, scourged, and bathed in blood, have mercy upon me and let me not faint in the fiery trial.

O Jesus, crowned with thorns and hailed in derision;

O Jesus, burdened with our sins and the curses of the people;

O Jesus, affronted, outraged, buffeted, overwhelmed with injuries, griefs, and humiliations;

O Jesus, hanging on the accursed tree, bowing the head, giving up the ghost, have mercy upon me and conform my whole soul to thy holy, humble, suffering Spirit.

O Thou who for the love of me hast undergone such an infinity of sufferings and humiliations, let me be wholly emptied of myself, that I may rejoice to take up my cross daily and follow thee.

HOLY, holy, holy, Lord God Almighty, I, miserable sinner, humbly acknowledge that I am altogether unworthy to pray for myself. But since thou hast commanded me to make prayers and intercessions for all men, in obedience to thy command and confidence of thy unlimited goodness, I commend to thy mercy the wants and necessities of all mankind.

HEAR, O merciful Father, my supplications, and that for the sake of thy Son, Jesus; and bring us, with all those who have pleased thee from the beginning of the world, into the glories of thy Son's kingdom, to whom with thee and the Holy Ghost be all praise forever and ever.

Friday Evening

O GOD the Father, who canst not be thought to have made me only to destroy me; have mercy upon me.

O God the Son, who, knowing thy Father's will didst come into the world to save me; have mercy upon me.

O God, the Holy Ghost, who to the same end hast
so often breathed holy thoughts into me; have mercy
upon me.

O holy, blessed, and glorious Trinity, whom in three
persons I adore as one God; have mercy upon me.

Save me, O God, as a brand snatched out of the fire.

Receive me, O my Saviour, as a sheep that is gone
astray but would now return to the great shepherd and
bishop of my soul.

Father, accept my imperfect repentance, compassionate my infirmities, forgive my wickedness, purify my
uncleanness, strengthen my weakness, fix my un-
stableness, and let thy good Spirit watch over me forever and thy love ever rule in my heart.

Give thy grace, O holy Jesus, to all the world, and let
all who are redeemed by thy blood acknowledge thee
to be the Lord. Let all Christians, especially those of
this nation, keep themselves unspotted from the world.
Let all rulers, and especially our Sovereign, rule with
wisdom and justice; and let the ministers of thy Church
be exemplary in their lives, and discreet and diligent

in their labors. Let our universities enjoy freedom from violence and faction, and excel in true religion and sound learning. Be a help at hand to all that are afflicted and assist them to trust in thee. Raise up friends for the widow and fatherless, the friendless and oppressed. Give patience to all that are sick, comfort to all troubled consciences, strength to all that are tempted.

BE gracious to my relations, to all that are endeared to me by their kindnesses or acquaintance, to all who remember me in their prayers or desire to be remembered in mine. Sanctify, O merciful Lord, the friendship which thou hast granted me with these thy servants. Let our prayers be heard for each other, while our hearts are united in thy fear and love; and graciously unite them therein more and more. Strengthen our hearts against all corruptions and temptations. Enable us to consecrate ourselves faithfully and entirely to thy service. Grant that we may provoke each other to love and serve thee, and grow up together before thee in thy fear and love to thy heavenly kingdom. And by thy infinite mercies vouchsafe to bring us, with those that are dead in thee, to rejoice together before thee, through the merits of our Lord Jesus Christ.

Saturday Morning

THOU art praised, O Lord, by all thy works and magnified by everything which thou hast created. The sun rejoiceth to run his course, that he may set forth thy praise who madest him. Nor do the moon and stars refrain to manifest thy glory, even amidst the silent night. The earth breathes forth fragrance, as incense to thee, her sacred king. The deep uttereth her voice, the floods clap their hands, and the hills are joyful together before thee.

THOU madest light for our comfort and broughtest forth darkness out of thy treasures to overshadow the earth, that the living creatures of it might take their rest. Fire and hail, snow and vapor, wind and storm, fulfill thy word and manifest thy glory. Suffer not the sons of men to be silent, but let the noblest work of thy creation pay thee the nobest sacrifice of praise.

POUR thy grace into my heart that I may worthily magnify thy great and glorious name. Thou hast made me and sent me into the world to do thy work. Assist me to fulfill the end of my creation and to show forth thy praise with all diligence by giving myself up to thy service. Prosper the work of my hands upon me,

O Lord. Prosper thou whatever I shall undertake this day, that it may tend to thy glory, the good of my neighbor, and the salvation of my own soul.

PRESERVE me from all those snares and temptations which continually solicit me to offend thee. Guide me by thy Holy Spirit in all those places whither thy providence shall lead me this day, and suffer not my communications with the world to dissipate my thoughts, to make me inadvertent to thy presence or lukewarm in thy service; but let me always walk as in thy sight and as one who knows this life to be the seedtime of an eternal harvest.

KEEP me, I beseech thee, undefiled, unblamable, and unreprovable unto the end; and grant that I may so diligently perform thy will in that station wherein thou hast been pleased to place me that I may make my calling and election sure, through Jesus Christ, our blessed Lord and Saviour.

HEAR also, O Lord, my prayers for the whole race of mankind, and guide their feet into the way of peace. Reform the corruptions of thy Church, heal her divisions, and restore to her her ancient discipline. Give to the ministers thereof grace as good shepherds to feed the flocks committed to their care. Bless the

King and all the royal family, and all that are put in
authority under him. Let them exceed others as much
in goodness as in greatness and be signal instruments
of thy glory. And keep, O Lord, all ranks of the people
of this land in constant communion with thy holy
Church, in humble obedience to the King, and in
Christian charity one toward another, through Jesus
Christ our Lord.

Saturday Evening

O MOST great and glorious God, who art mighty in thy
power and wonderful in thy doings toward the sons
of men; accept, I beseech thee, my unfeigned thanks
and praise for my creation, preservation, and all the
other blessings which in the riches of thy mercy thou
hast from time to time poured down upon me.

THOU hast instructed us by thy laws and enlightened
us by thy statutes. Thou hast redeemed us by the blood
of thy son and sanctified us by the grace of thy Holy
Spirit. For these and all thy other mercies how can I
ever sufficiently love thee or worthily magnify thy
great and glorious name? All the powers of my soul

are too few to conceive the thanks that are due to thee.

BUT thou hast declared thou wilt accept the sacrifice of thanksgiving in return for all thy goodness. Forever therefore will I bless thee, will I adore thy power and magnify thy goodness. My tongue shall sing of thy righteousness and be telling of thy salvation from day to day. I will give thanks unto thee forever and ever; I will praise my God while I have my being.

THOUGH I am upon earth, yet will I praise, as I can, the King of heaven. Though a mortal creature, yet will I join my song with the immortal host of angels and archangels, thrones, dominions, and powers, while they laud and magnify thy glorious name.

Holy, holy, holy, is the Lord of hosts! Heaven and earth are full of his glory! Glory be to thee, O Lord most high.

ACCEPT, O merciful Father, my most humble thanks for thy preservation of me this day. Continue thy lovingkindness toward me, and take me into thy protection this night. Let thy holy angels watch over me and defend me from evil men and evil spirits. Let me rest in peace and not sleep in sin, and grant that I may rise more fit for thy service.

O THOU whose kingdom ruleth over all, rule in the hearts of all the men whom thou hast made. Reform the corruptions and heal the breaches of thy holy Church, and establish her in truth and peace. Be gracious unto the ministers of thy gospel and give them rightly to divide the word of truth. Forgive the sins of this nation and turn our hearts, that iniquity may not be our ruin.

BE gracious to all who are near and dear to me. Thou knowest their names and art acquainted with their wants. Of thy goodness be pleased to proportion thy blessings to their necessities. Pardon my enemies, and give them repentance and charity, and me grace to overcome evil with good. Have compassion on all who are distressed in mind, body, or estate; give them steady patience and timely deliverance.

O LORD, thou God of spirits and of all flesh, be mindful of thy faithful. And for thy Son's sake give to them and us in thy due time a happy resurrection and a glorious rest at thy right hand forevermore.

Now, to God the Father, who first loved us and made us accepted in the beloved; to God the Son, who loved us and washed us from our sins; to God the Holy Ghost, who sheddeth the love of God abroad in our hearts; be all love and all glory in time and to all eternity.

FAMILY PRAYERS

FOR EACH DAY of the WEEK

Sunday Morning

ALMIGHTY and eternal God, we desire to praise thy holy name for so graciously raising us up in soundness of body and mind to see the light of this day.

WE bless thee in behalf of all thy creatures; for the eyes of all look unto thee, and thou givest them their meat in due season. But, above all, we acknowledge thy inestimable benefits bestowed upon mankind in Christ Jesus. We thank thee for his miraculous birth, for his most holy life, his bitter agony and death, for his glorious resurrection, his ascension into heaven, his triumph over all the powers of darkness, and his sitting at thy right hand forevermore.

O GOD, how great was thy love to the sinful sons of men!

OH, THE riches of thy grace in sending the Holy Spirit to make us abound in hope, that we shall one day rise from the dead and after our short labors here rest with thee in thy eternal glory!

WE would begin this day in devout meditations, in joy unspeakable, and in blessing and praising thee, who hast given us such good hope and everlasting consolation. Lift up our minds above all these little things below, which are apt to distract our thoughts; and keep them above till our hearts are fully bent to seek thee every day in the way wherein Jesus hath gone before us.

WE are ashamed, O Lord, to think that ever we have disobeyed thee, who hast redeemed us by the precious blood of thine own Son. Oh, that we may agree with thy will in all things for the time to come! And that all the powers of our souls and bodies may be wholly dedicated to thy service! We desire unfeignedly that all the thoughts and designs of our minds, all the affections and tempers of our hearts, and all the actions of our lives may be pure, holy, and unreprovable in thy sight.

SEARCH us, O Lord, and prove us. Look well if there be any way of wickedness in us, and lead us in the way everlasting. Let thy favor be better to us than life itself, that so in all things we may approve our hearts before thee and feel the sense of thy acceptance of us, giving us a joy which the world cannot give.

O LORD, hear us and make thy face to shine upon us, that we may enter into thy gates with thanksgiving and into thy courts with praise, that we may be thankful unto thee and bless thy name, for Jesus Christ's sake, in whose words we conclude our imperfect prayers, saying: *Our Father, ...*

Sunday Evening

O THOU high and holy One that inhabitest eternity, thou art to be feared and loved by all thy servants. All thy works praise thee, O God, and we especially give thanks unto thee for thy marvelous love in Christ Jesus, by whom thou hast reconciled the world to thyself. Thou hast given us exceeding great and precious promises. Thou hast sealed them with his blood. Thou hast confirmed them by his resurrection and ascension, and the coming of the Holy Ghost. We thank thee that thou hast given us so many happy opportunities of knowing the truth as it is in Jesus, even the mystery which was hid from ages and generations, but is now revealed to them that believe.

BLESSED be thy goodness for the great consolation and assistance of thy Holy Spirit. Blessed be thy goodness, that we have felt it so often in our hearts, inspiring us with holy thoughts, filling us with love, joy, and comfortable expectations of the glory that shall be revealed.

WE offer up again our souls and bodies to thee, to be governed, not by our own will, but thine. Let it ever be the ease and joy of our hearts to be under the conduct of thy unerring wisdom, to follow thy counsels, and to be ruled in all things by thy holy will. And let us never distrust thy abundant kindness and tender care over us whatsoever it is thou wouldst have us to do or to suffer in this world.

O GOD, purify our hearts that we may entirely love thee and rejoice in being loved of thee; that we may confide in thee, and absolutely resign ourselves to thee and be filled with constant devotion toward thee; that we may never sink into a base love of anything here below nor be oppressed with the cares of this life; but assist us to abhor that which is evil and cleave to that which is good. Give us true humility of spirit that we may not think of ourselves more highly than we ought to think. Keep us from being wise in our own conceits. Let our moderation be known to all men.

COMPOSE our spirits to a quiet and steady dependence on thy good providence.

SEND forth thy light and thy truth into all the dark corners of the earth, that all kings may fall down before thee and all nations do thee service. Bless these kingdoms, and give us grace at length to bring forth fruits meet for repentance. O Lord, save the King and establish his throne in righteousness. Prosper the endeavors of all who faithfully feed thy people and increase the number of them, that the seed which hath been sown this day may take deep root in all our hearts; that, being not forgetful hearers but doers of the word, we may be blessed in our deeds.

HELP us in all this week following to set a watch before our mouths and keep the door of our lips. And let not our hearts incline to any evil thing or to practice wicked works with men that work iniquity. But as we have received how we ought to walk and to please thee, so may we abound more and more.

PROTECT us, we beseech thee, and all our friends everywhere this night, and awaken in the morning those good thoughts in our hearts, that the words of our Saviour may abide in us and we in him, who hath taught us when we pray to say: *Our Father, . . .*

Monday Morning

WE humble ourselves, O Lord of heaven and earth, before thy glorious majesty. We acknowledge thy eternal power, wisdom, goodness, and truth, and desire to render unto thee most unfeigned thanks for all the benefits which thou pourest upon us. But, above all, for thine inestimable love in the redemption of the world by our Lord Jesus Christ.

WE implore thy tender mercies in the forgiveness of all our sins whereby we have offended either in thought, word, or deed. We desire to be truly sorry for all our misdoings and utterly to renounce whatsoever is contrary to thy will. We desire to devote our whole man body, soul, and spirit, to thee. And as thou dost inspire us with these desires, so accompany them always with thy grace, that we may every day with our whole hearts give ourselves up to thy service.

THOU hast mercifully kept us the last night; blessed be thy continued goodness. Receive us likewise into thy protection this day. Guide and assist us in all our thoughts, words, and actions. Make us willing to do and suffer what thou pleasest, waiting for the mercy of our Lord Jesus Christ unto eternal life.

LET us abound in thy love more and more, and in continual prayers and praises to thee, the Father of mercies and God of all consolation, in Jesus Christ our Lord.

AND we desire the good of all mankind, especially of all Christian people, that they may walk worthy of the gospel and live together in unity and Christian love.

BLESS all those that watch over our souls; succeed their labors and give us grace to follow their godly admonitions.

THE same blessings we crave for our friends, relations, and acquaintances, that we may all live in perfect love and peace together, and rejoice together at the great day of the Lord Jesus, in whose holy words we sum up all our wants: *Our Father, . . .*

Monday Evening

ALMIGHTY and most merciful Father, in whom we live, move, and have our being; to whose tender compassions we owe our safety the day that is past, together with all the comforts of this life and the hopes of that which is to come; we praise thee, O Lord. We bow ourselves before thee, acknowledging we have nothing but what we receive from thee. Unto thee do we give thanks, O God, who daily pourest thy benefits upon us.

BLESSED be thy goodness for our health, for our food and raiment, for our peace and safety, for the love of our friends, for all our blessings in this life and our desire to attain that life which is immortal. Blessed be thy love for that we feel in our hearts any motion toward thee.

BEHOLD, O Lord, we present ourselves before thee to be inspired with such a vigorous sense of thy love as may put us forward with a greater earnestness, zeal, and diligence in all our duty. Renew in us, we beseech thee, a lively image of thee in all righteousness, purity, mercy, faithfulness, and truth, that Jesus, the hope of glory, may be formed in us.

GUIDE us safely through all the changes of this life in an unchangeable love to thee and a lively sense of thy love to us, till we come to live with thee and enjoy thee forever.

AND now, as we lay ourselves down to sleep, take us into thy gracious protection and settle our spirits in quiet thoughts of thy glory.

To thy blessing we commend all mankind, high and low, rich and poor, that they may all faithfully serve thee and contentedly enjoy whatsoever is needful for them.

AND when we awake in the morning, may we praise thee again with joyful lips and still offer ourselves a more acceptable sacrifice to thee, through Jesus Christ, in whose words we beseech thee to hear us, according to the full sense and meaning thereof: *Our Father, . . .*

Tuesday Morning

O MOST great and mighty God, the possessor of heaven
and earth, all the angels rejoice in blessing and praising
thee, the Father of spirits; for thou hast created all
things, and in wisdom hast thou made them all.

SINCE at the best we are unprofitable servants and can
do no more than it is our duty to do, enable us to do
everything which thou hast commanded us, heartily,
with good will and true love to thy service.

RENDER us so mindful of the great love of our Lord
that we may be zealously concerned for his glory and
use our utmost diligence to commemorate his death and
passion, making a joyful sacrifice of our souls and
bodies to him, and earnestly desiring that his kingdom
may come over all the earth.

Fulfill, most merciful Lord, all our petitions; and
as thou hast graciously protected us this night, so accompany us all this day with thy blessing.

GRANT that all men may be awakened into a lively
and thankful sense of all thy benefits. Stir up especially the minds of all Christian people to follow the

truth as it is in Jesus and exercise themselves to have a conscience void of offense toward God and toward man. May true religion, justice, mercy, brotherly kindness, and all things else that are praiseworthy so flourish among us that we may enjoy the blessings of peace and plenty, and that there may be no complaining in our streets.

O GOD, whose never-failing providence ordereth all things both in heaven and earth; keep us, we beseech thee, from all hurtful things, and give us those things which are profitable for us, according to thine abundant mercy in our Lord Jesus, in whose words we conclude our supplications, saying: *Our Father, . . .*

Tuesday Evening

WE pray thee to increase every good desire which we feel already in our hearts. Let us live always as becomes the disciples of Jesus Christ. Incline us to be more and more in love with thy laws till they are written upon our hearts. Stir up our wills to love them exceedingly and to cleave unto them as our very life.

MAY there ever abide in us such a strong and powerful sense of thy mighty love toward us in Christ Jesus as may constrain us freely and willingly to please thee in the constant exercise of righteousness and mercy, temperance and charity, meekness and patience, truth and fidelity, together with such a humble, contented, and peaceable spirit as may adorn the religion of our Lord and Master.

MAY the example of our blessed Saviour be always dear to us, that we may cheerfully follow him in every holy temper and delight to do thy will, O God. Let these desires which thou hast given us never die or languish in our hearts, but be kept always alive in their vigor and force by the perpetual inspirations of the Holy Ghost.

ACCEPT likewise our thanks for thy merciful preservation of us this day. We are bold again to commit ourselves unto thee this night. Defend us from all the powers of darkness, and raise us up in the morning to such a vigorous sense of thy continual goodness as may provoke us all the day long to an unwearied diligence in well-doing.

AND the same mercies that we beg for ourselves we desire for the rest of mankind, especially for those who are called by the name of Christ; and that every one of these may do his duty with fidelity. *Our Father, . . .*

Wednesday Morning

O GOD, blessed forever, we thank and praise thee for all thy benefits, for the comforts of this life and our hope of everlasting salvation in the life to come.

THOU hast delivered thine own Son for us all. How shalt thou not with him also freely give us all things?

WE depend upon thee, especially for the grace of thy Holy Spirit. May we feel it perpetually bearing us up, by the strength of our most holy faith, above all the temptations that may at any time assault us.

LET thy mighty power enable us to do our duty toward thee and toward all men with care, diligence, zeal, and perseverance unto the end. Help us to be meek and gentle in our conversation, prudent and discreet in ordering our affairs, observant of thy fatherly providence in everything that befalls us, thankful for thy benefits, patient under thy chastisements, and readily disposed for every good word and work.

DELIVER us, we beseech thee, from worldly cares and
foolish desires, from vain hopes and causeless fears,
and so dispose our hearts that death itself may not be
dreadful to us.

MAY our hearts be so firmly established in grace that
nothing may affright us or shake our constancy.

WE commend unto thee all mankind. Bless our Sovereign, his counselors and ministers and all employed in
public business, whether spiritual or civil, that whatsoever they do may be for thy glory and the public
good.

BE gracious unto all that are near and dear to us, and
keep us all in thy fear and love. Guide us, good Lord,
and govern us by the same Spirit, that we may be so
united to thee here as not to be divided when thou art
pleased to call us hence, but may together enter into
thy glory, through Jesus Christ, our blessed Lord and
Saviour, who hath taught us when we pray to say:
Our Father, . . .

Wednesday Evening

O LORD, how manifold are thy works! In wisdom hast thou made them all. The day is thine; the night also is thine; thou hast prepared the light and the sun. We render thee thanks for all the benefits which thou hast bestowed on the whole world, especially on us whom thou hast called to the knowledge of thy grace in Christ Jesus.

ACCEPT, O merciful Father, the good resolutions which thou hast inspired us with by thy Spirit. Strengthen them, we beseech thee, with thy continued grace, that no sudden desires, vehement inclinations, ineffectual purposes, or partial performances may lead us into a false opinion of ourselves, but that we may bring forth actually and with a constant spirit all the fruits of righteousness which are by Christ Jesus.

LIFT our affections to things above, that we may have perfect contentment in well-doing and patient suffering. Free us from the cares of this world, from all distrust of thy good providence, from repining at anything that befalls us; and enable us in everything to give thanks, believing that all things are ordered wisely and shall work together for our good.

INTO thy hands we commend both our souls and bodies which thou hast mercifully preserved this day. We trust in thy watchful providence who givest thy angels charge over us. Continue these holy thoughts and desires in us till we fall asleep, that we may receive the light of morning with a new joy in thee and thankful affection to thee.

WE desire likewise, O God, the good of the whole world. Pity the follies of mankind; deliver them from their miseries and forgive thou all their sins. Hear the cry of every part of the creation and bring them all into the glorious liberty of the sons of God.

HEAR the daily prayers of the Church. Free her from error. Let the truth as it is in Jesus prevail and peace be in all her borders.

STRENGTHEN all thy faithful servants. Bring back them that wander out of the way. Raise up those that are fallen. Confirm those that stand, and grant them steadily to persevere in faith, love, and obedience. Relieve and comfort all that are in distress. Let the earth bring forth her fruit in due season, and let all honest and industrious people be blest in their labors. Remember all those who have done good unto us. Grant forgiveness and charity to all our enemies, and continue good will among all our neighbors. Support the sick with faith and patience. Assist those who are leaving this world. Receive the souls which thou hast redeemed, and give us all a glorious resurrection and eternal life. *Our Father, . . .*

Thursday Morning

O Lord, the God of our salvation, thou art the hope of the ends of the earth. Upon thee the eyes of all do wait, for thou givest unto all, life, and breath, and all things. Thou still watchest over us for good; thou daily renewest to us our lives and thy mercies; and thou hast given us the assurance of thy word that if we commit our affairs to thee, if we acknowledge thee in all our ways, thou wilt direct our paths.

We desire, O Lord, to be still under thy gracious conduct and fatherly protection. We beg the guidance and help of thy good Spirit to dispose of us and all that concerns us to the glory of thy name.

O Lord, withdraw not thy tender mercies from us, nor
the comforts of thy presence. Pardon all our sins, and
save us from all our iniquities.

Sanctify to us all our employments in the world, our
crosses also, and our comforts, all the estates we go
through, and all the events that befall us.

Gracious Father, keep us, we pray thee, this day in thy
fear and favor, and teach us in all our thoughts, words
and works to live to thy glory. If thou guide us not
we go astray; if thou uphold us not, we fall. Let thy
good providence be our defense and thy good Spirit
our guide and counselor, and supporter in all our ways.
And grant that we may do always what is acceptable in
thy sight, through Jesus Christ our Lord, in whose holy
name we close these our imperfect prayers: *Our Father*
. . .

Let thy grace, O Lord Jesus; thy love, O heavenly
Father; and thy comfortable fellowship, O blessed
Spirit, be with us and all who desire our prayers this
day and forevermore.

Thursday Evening

O Lord, thy glory is above all our thoughts and thy mercy is over all thy works.

Thou hast sent thy only Son that whosoever believeth in him should not perish but have everlasting life. O Lord, we believe; help our unbelief. Give us true repentance toward God and faith in our Lord Jesus Christ, and let the love of God be shed abroad in our hearts by the Holy Ghost which is given us.

Thou knowest, O Lord, all our temptations and the sin which doth so easily beset us. Thou knowest the devices of the enemy and the deceitfulness of our own hearts. We pray thee, good Lord, that thou wilt arm us with the whole armor of God. Uphold us with thy free spirit and watch over us for good evermore.

Let our supplications also ascend before thee for the whole race of mankind. Send thy word unto all the ends of the earth, and let it be the savor of life unto all that hear it.

Be gracious to this our native land. Do thou rule all our rulers, counsel all our counselors, teach all our teachers, and order all the public affairs to thy glory. Turn from

us the judgments which we feel or fear. Continue th
blessings to our souls and bodies. And notwithstandin
all our provocations be thou still our God and let us b
thy people.

BE gracious to all our friends and neighbors. Bless ou
relations with the best of thy blessings, with thy fea
and love. Preserve us from our enemies, and reconcil
them both to us and to thyself.

LET thy blessing rest upon us of this family. In ever
condition secure our hearts to thyself, and make u
ever to approve ourselves sincere and faithful in th
service.

AND now, O Father of mercies, be pleased to accept ou
evening sacrifice of praise and thanksgiving. Imprir
and preserve upon our hearts a lively sense of all th
kindness to us, that our souls may bless thee and a
that is within us may praise thy holy name.

FOR all thy patience with us, thy care over us, and th
continual mercy to us blessed be thy name, O Lor
God, our heavenly Father. And unto thee, with the So
of thy love and the Spirit of grace, be all thanks an
praise now and forevermore. *Our Father, . . .*

Friday Morning

How excellent is thy lovingkindness, O God! The children of men shall put their trust under the shadow of thy wings.

Look not upon the sin of our nature nor the sins of our hearts and lives, which are more than we can remember and greater than we can express. It is of the Lord's mercies that we are not consumed, because thy compassions fail not.

O God, be merciful to us for his sake whom thou hast exalted to be a Prince and a Saviour, to give repentance unto thy people and forgiveness of sins. Be merciful unto our souls which have greatly sinned. Heal our backslidings; renew us to repentance. Establish our hearts in thy fear and love, and establish our goings in thy way that our footsteps slip not. Let us waver no more. Let us nevermore be weary or faint in our minds. Let us not revolt from thee or turn to folly again after thou hast spoken peace to our souls, but may we go on conquering and to conquer all the enemies of our souls and all the hindrances of our salvation, till thou hast bruised Satan under our feet.

SEEING there is in Christ Jesus an infinite fullness of al
that we can want or wish, may we receive of his fullnes
grace upon grace: grace to pardon our sins and subdu
our iniquities; to justify our persons and to sanctify ou
souls; and to complete that holy change, that renewa
of heart, whereby we may be transformed into tha
blessed image wherein thou didst create us. So make u
all meet to be partakers of the inheritance of thy saint
in light.

AND teach us, O God, to use this world without abusing
it and to receive the things needful for the body with
out losing our part in thy love. Whatever we have i
this world, may we have the same with thy leave an
love, sanctified to us by the word of God and by prayer
and by the right improvement thereof to thy glory. An
whatever we want of worldly things, leave us not desti
tute of the things that accompany salvation, but ador
our souls with all such graces of thy Holy Spirit tha
we may adorn the doctrine of our God and Saviour i
all things.

AND now that thou hast renewed our lives and th
mercies to us this morning, help us to renew our desire
resolutions, and endeavors to live in obedience to th
holy will. Restrain us from the sins into which we ar

most prone to fall, and quicken us to the duties we are most averse to perform. And grant that we may think and speak, and will and do, the things becoming the children of our heavenly Father, and so find the strong consolation of thy gracious acceptance in Jesus Christ our Saviour, who, when we pray, hath taught us to say: *Our Father, . . .*

Friday Evening

O LORD, thou wast before all, thou art above all, and thy years shall not fail. Thou art the searcher of our hearts. Thou knowest the dullness and hardness, the vanity and deceitfulness of them. We were born sinners and have added sin to sin. We have abused thy great and manifold mercies, tempted thy patience, and despised thy goodness.

BUT of thy lovingkindnesses there is no number. Thou still callest us to return to thee, and whosoever cometh unto thee, thou wilt in no wise cast out. O meet us with thy heavenly grace that we may be able to come to thee. Stretch forth thy hand and loose the chains wherewith our souls are entangled. Free us from every weight of sin, from every yoke of bondage. Help us to feel, be-

wail, and forsake all our sins. And let us never want
the comfortable assurance of thy forgiveness of them,
thy acceptance of us, and thy love to us, in the blessed
Son of thy eternal love.

THOU art never weary, O Lord, of doing us good. Let
us never be weary of doing thee service. Let us take
pleasure in thy service and abound in thy work and in
thy love and praise evermore. Fill up all that is wanting,
reform whatever is amiss in us, perfect the thing that
concerneth us, and let the witness of thy pardoning love
ever abide in all our hearts.

BLESS to us whatsoever thou art pleased to allot to us,
and everything that befalls us. May all work together
for good to build us up in thy grace and to help us on to
thy glory.

CONTINUE thy fatherly care over us this night; preserve,
defend, bless, and keep us, that no evil may befall us,
nor any plague come nigh our dwelling. Give us comfortable sleep to strengthen us for thy service. And for
all that Jesus Christ hath done and suffered for us, to
thy name, O blessed God of our salvation, be the praise
and honor and glory, now and forever. *Our Father, . . .*

Saturday Morning

WE present ourselves before thee, O Lord our God, to pay our tribute of praise and thanksgiving, desiring thee mercifully to accept us and our services at the hands of Jesus Christ. In his great name we come to beg thy pardon and peace, the increase of thy grace and tokens of thy love; for we are not worthy of the least of thy mercies. But worthy is the Lamb that was slain to take away the sin of the world, for whose sake thou wilt give us all things.

O MERCIFUL FATHER, regard not what we have done against thee but what our blessed Saviour hath done for us. Regard not what we have made ourselves but what he is made unto us of thee. Teach us to know thee, O God, and Jesus Christ, whom thou hast sent. And enable us to do thy will on earth as it is done in heaven. Give us to fear thee and to love thee and to cleave to thee with full purpose of heart, that no temptations may draw or drive us from thee but that all thy dispensations toward us and thy dealings with us may be the messengers of thy love to our souls.

QUICKEN us, O Lord, in our dullness, that we may not serve thee in a lifeless and listless manner but may abound in thy work and be fervent in spirit, serving the Lord.

MAKE us faithful in all our intercourse with our neigh bor, that we may be ready to do good and bear evil that we may be just and kind, merciful and meek peaceable and patient, sober and temperate, humble and self-denying, inoffensive and useful in the world; that so glorifying thee here, we may be glorified with thee in thy heavenly kingdom.

DAY by day we magnify thee, O Lord, who makes every day an addition to thy mercies. We bless thee fo preserving us the night past and for the rest thou gaves us therein. Oh, cause us to hear thy lovingkindness in the morning, for in thee do we trust. Cause us to know the way wherein we shall go, for we lift up our soul unto thee. Take not thy Holy Spirit from us but direc all our ways to please thee.

HELP us to see thy power, to own thy presence, to ad mire thy wisdom, and to love thy goodness in all th creatures; and by all draw our hearts still nearer to thee Such mercy and grace we beg for ourselves, and all our and thine everywhere, in our great Mediator's blesse words: *Our Father, . . .*

Saturday Evening

O LORD our God, thou art infinitely good, and thou hast showed us what is good. Thou sendest out thy light and thy truth that they may guide us and makest plain thy way before our face. Thou givest us many opportunities to quicken and further us in thy service. Thou hast called, and we have refused. Thou hast stretched forth thy hands, and we have not regarded. And our iniquities become our ruin.

O LORD, enter not into judgment with thy servants. Pardon all our contempt of thy word and our not profiting thereby. And help us for the time to come better to improve the blessed opportunities set before us.

As the rain descends from heaven and returns not thither but waters the earth and maketh it fruitful, so let not thy word return unto thee void but prosper in the work whereunto thou sendest it. Make it effectual to build us all up in the true fear and love of God, and in the knowledge and faith of our Lord Jesus Christ.

WE beg thy gracious acceptance of our humble praise and thanksgiving for all thy blessings, spiritual and temporal, so freely conferred upon us. We praise thee for all the comforts and conveniences of this life and for all the means and hopes of a better, particularly for what we have received this day: the food of our souls set before us, the word of salvation sounding in our ears, and thy Spirit striving with our hearts. Withdraw not thy tender mercies from us but still continue thy accustomed goodness, increase thy grace and heavenly blessings upon us, and rejoice over us to do us good.

In mercy pass by all which thy most pure and holy eyes have seen amiss in us this day. Forgive the iniquities of our holy things; overlook all our sins and failings, through our great Mediator and Redeemer, who ever lives at thy right hand to make intercession for us. And for Jesus Christ and for all which thou art pleased to give us together with him, not unto us but unto thy name be all the praise and honor and glory humbly ascribed by us and all thy Church, now and forevermore. *Our Father, . . .*

DEVOTIONS *for*
EVERY DAY *of the* WEEK

Sunday

PREVENT, we beseech thee, O Lord, all our doings with thy most gracious inspirations, and further them with thy continual help, that every prayer and work of ours may begin always from thee and by thee be happily ended, and more especially the service we are now entering upon, through Jesus Christ our Lord.

This is the day which the Lord hath made; let us be glad and rejoice therein.

This is the day he hath sanctified to himself and called by his own most holy name:

That in it we may meet to adore his greatness and admire the wonders of his infinite power:

That we may remember his innumerable mercies and deeply imprint them in our hearts:

That we may visit his holy temple and humbly present our homage at his altar:

That sacred altar, where the sacrifice of the Lamb of God is shown forth and the memory of our Saviour's love continually renewed.

O GLORIOUS Jesus, in whom we live and without whom we die; mortify in us all sensual desires and quicken our hearts with thy holy love, that we may no longer esteem the vanities of the world, but place our affections entirely on thee, who didst die for our sins and rise again for our justification.

Oh, how adorable are thy counsels, O Lord! How strangely endearing the ways of thy love!

Raise thy head, O my soul, and look up and behold the glory of thy crucified Saviour.

He is risen and made the light his garment and commanded the clouds to be the chariot of his triumph.

O glorious Jesus, our strength, our joy, and the immortal life of our souls!

O GOD, who hast glorified our victorious Saviour with a visible triumphant resurrection from the dead and ascension into heaven, where he sits at thy right hand; grant, we beseech thee, that his triumphs and glories may ever shine in our eyes, to make us more clearly see through his sufferings and more courageously endure our own; being assured by his example that if we endeavor to live and die like him for the advancement of thy love in ourselves and others, thou wilt raise again our dead bodies and, conforming them to his glorious body, call us above the clouds and give us possession of thy everlasting kingdom; through the same Lord Jesus Christ, thy Son, who, with thee and the Holy Ghost, liveth and reigneth one God, world without end.

Make me still think on my country above, and there establish my eternal home.

If these imperfect shadows so sweetly please, how will the real substance transport our hearts!

Blessed be thy gracious wisdom, O Lord, that so mercifully stoops to our low conceptions.

All is unquiet here till we come to thee and repose at last in the kingdom of peace.

Blessed be the holy name of the Lord our God who hath showed us the light of his countenance and hath caused us to see his goodness in the land of the living. For, behold, thou art the light of the nations, O Christ, and the glory of thy Church.

LORD, we beseech thee, forsake us not in the vanishing of our days; but still continue thy gracious and fatherly protection unto us. Be thou our light and defense, our guide and guard, through the valley of misery and tears, and the shadow of death, to that holy hill where thine honor and our rest dwelleth. And give us the peace and comfort and communion of thy Holy Spirit, that our eyes may see thy salvation, and we thy servants may depart in thy peace, for the merits and satisfaction of thy dear Son, Jesus Christ our Lord.

May our minds never be discomposed with passion, nor our tongues break forth into violent expressions; but may our temper be always preserved calm and regular, and as becomes all those whose powers are possessed of the joys of heaven, apt to feel in everything only the sweet impulses of hope and charity, through our Lord Jesus Christ thy Son, to whom, with thee and the Holy Ghost, be all honor and glory, world without end.

Vouchsafe us, we beseech thee, O Lord, a quiet night and a happy end.

Visit, we beseech thee, O Lord, this habitation, and drive far away all snares of the enemy. Let thy holy angels dwell therein to preserve us in peace, and thy blessing be upon us forever, through our Lord Jesus Christ, thy Son.

Monday

Let us with reverence appear before him and humble ourselves in the presence of his glory. For himself he made us and for his glorious kingdom.

GUIDE me with thy holy grace, that I may withdraw my affections from all vain and perishable creatures, and fix them entirely on thee, my Lord and my God.

Send down, O God of our fathers and Lord of mercy, thy wisdom from thy holy heaven and from the seat of thy greatness, to be in us, and labor with us, and teach us what is acceptable unto thee; that we may know our end, and wisely choose our way, and order our actions to our true felicity. Our thoughts are fearful and our prudence uncertain; we scarce conjecture the things that are on earth and find with pains the things that are in sight. Give us, O Lord, the wisdom that sits at thy throne and reject us not from among thy children.

Deliver us, O Lord, from relapsing into the sins we have repented of.

Thou art our strength, O Lord; whom shall we fear? Thou art our salvation; of what shall we be afraid? Nothing can hurt us but our own vicious desires; nothing can endanger us but disobedience to our God.

O God, who art ever present to all that thou hast made, still watching to improve us as we grow fit for greater bounty; keep, we beseech thee, our eyes continually fixed on thine over us, checking our inclination to folly and encouraging our pursuit of true good.

Thou art worthy, O Lord, to receive glory and honor and power, for thou hast created all things, and for thy pleasure they are and were created.

To know thee, O Lord, is the highest learning, and to see thy face the only happiness.

Suffer us not to go till thou hast given us thy blessing, and then may thy blessing bind us faster unto thee.

He that framed the heart of man, designed it for himself, and bequeathed it unquietness till possessed of its Maker.

All thy ways, O Lord, are mercy and wisdom, and all thy counsels tend to our happiness.

Tuesday

Not unto us, O Lord, not unto us, but to thine own blessed name give all the glory.

Every moment of our day subsists by thee, and every step we take moves by thy strength.

Fix thou our steps, O Lord, that we stagger not at the uneven motions of the world, but steadily go on to our glorious home, neither censuring our journey by the weather we meet with, nor turning out of the way for anything that befalls us.

O God, the eternal source and necessity of being, on whose free overflowing that of the whole creation every moment depends! Strike, we beseech thee, our hearts with a continual dread and reverence of thy absolute dominion, which should it but never so little suspend thy bounty, we should instantly vanish into nothing; and grant that we may by thy grace so husband our time here as in the next life to possess thy eternity, through our Lord Jesus Christ.

Be thou eternally adored, O God of our salvation, and may thy praises be sung by thy servants forever.

O blessed Jesus, our strength and our guide, who knowest and pitiest our weak capacities,

Who in thy tender care hast contrived such means that nothing can undo us but our own perverseness.

Rejoice, and with your bended knees and hearts adore the blessed Jesus.

He came with his hands full of miracles, and every miracle full of mercies.

One miracle more we humbly beg, but one as strange and hard as any of the rest:

Soften our stony hearts into a tender sense of thy great goodness and their own true duty.

He founded his Church on an immovable rock, to render our faith firm and secure.

He sealed his love with sacraments of grace, to breed and nourish up in us the life of love.

If we forget thee, thou renewest our memory; if we fly from thee, thou still findest means to recall us.

If we defer our amendment, thou patiently stayest for us; and when we return, thou openest thy arms to embrace us.

We know thy ways are in the deep abyss, and none can sound the bottom of thy counsels.

Yet may we safely look on the flowing streams and gather this comfort from their gentle course.

When we were not, thou freely lovedst us; thou wilt not forsake us now we strive to love thee.

When we had lost our way, thou soughtest after us; thou wilt not refuse us now we seek after thee.

We who are bought by the blood of Jesus and freely redeemed by his sacred Cross!

Shall we neglect so gracious a Saviour, whose only design is to draw us to his love?

*May thy holy will be all our rule and thy gracious
hand our only guide.*

O GRACIOUS GOD, may we feel ourselves confounded
with shame at our notorious follies and be henceforth
apter to learn by all the world about us our duty to
thee, through our Lord Jesus Christ.

Wednesday

*He is our great and sovereign Lord, the absolute king
of heaven and earth; he sees at once the whole frame
of all things and thoroughly comprehends their various
natures.*

*To every creature he appoints a fit office and guides
all their motions in perfect order, till he has wrought
his glorious design to finish the world in a beauteous
close.*

*All these he governs by his infinite wisdom and all
for the good of them that love him; his counsels are
deep and beyond our reach, but all his ways are just
and merciful.*

*The day will come, it will infallibly come, when God
will crown all that love his glory.*

*Let us not faint, and we shall surely see a prosperous
issue of all our sorrows.*

O Lord, bow down thy gracious eye and pity the frail
ties of our imperfect nature. Reach forth thy hand and
strengthen us with thy grace, that nothing may divert
our advance toward thee. But in this dangerous laby
rinth of the world and the whole course of our pilgrim
age here, thy heavenly dictates be our map and thy
holy life be our guide.

*May every age sing praises to our God and all genera
tions adore his providence.*

*Blessed be thy goodness, O gracious God, who hast
thus made known thy will to us.*

*Blessed be thy power, O Lord, who by thy apostle
hast wrought such miracles to confirm thy faith and
inclined our hearts to believe it.*

*Lord, how secure and quiet they live, whom thy
grace preserves in innocence!*

*The day goes smoothly over their heads and silent
as the shadow of a dial.*

*Their spirits run calm and even, and ebb and flow
in obedience to reason.*

*Till some unruly passion presses to come in and by its
fawning outside gains admittance.*

*Soon it grows bold to undermine their repose and
open a door to all their enemies.*

So at a little breach of the city wall a whole army pours in.

Send down thy powerful grace to sustain us and thoroughly reduce these unquiet disorders.

Govern all our senses, that they seduce not our mind; and order every motion of our heart.

Perfect the work thou hast begun and make our passions the servants of thy grace.

THE winds are often rough, and our own weight presses us downward.

Reach forth, O Lord, thy hand, thy saving hand, and speedily deliver us.

O GOD, whose grace it is that mightily rescues our reason from the desperate rebellion of our passions; grant, we beseech thee, that the experience of the miserable effects of yielding to their allurements may make us warier in observing and severer in repressing their first motions; and let thy grace so strongly fortify us against all their assaults that reason may more and more recover its due force and calmly join with faith to secure and exalt in our hearts the blissful throne of thy love, through our Lord Jesus Christ, thy Son, who liveth and reigneth with thee and the Holy Ghost, one God, blessed forever.

Grace gives us faith to fortify our reason, and heaven itself shall be conquered by us.

Thursday

He freely opens his bounteous hand and fills with his blessings every living creature.

He feeds our understanding with the knowledge of truth and strengthens our wills with his holy grace.

With himself and his sacred body and blood he feeds us and nourishes us up to immortal life.

May the faith which was once delivered to the saints continue in a happy progress to the end of all things.

Every station of our pilgrimage has a fit entertainment and every defect a proper remedy.

Behold he comes to us in the symbols of bread and wine, who is indeed both God and man.

BEHOLD, O Lord, we believe; perfect by thy vigorous grace our faint endeavors.

Bring us where our dark faith shall cease into vision and our hope expire into full enjoyment,

Where all our affections shall be contracted into love and love shall be extended to all eternity.

Blessed are the eyes, O Jesus, that see thee in these holy signs; and blessed is the mouth that reverently receives thee.

Blessed yet more is the heart that desires thy coming.

O BOUNTEOUS LORD, the continual supplier of thy creatures with all convenient sustenance to advance our growth and strength, till we are fit to take heaven by violence and rise at length to be eternal enjoyers of thyself; fix, we beseech thee, our eyes and adoration on that open hand, which thus graciously gives us our daily bread. And grant that the wonderful feast of thy Son's body and blood may duly sanctify our tastes to all other of thy bounties, that they may only relish and feed upon thy dear love to us, through the same our Lord Jesus Christ.

Whither, O my God, should we wander if left to ourselves? Where should we fix our hearts if not directed by thee?

Thou didst send forth thy Holy Spirit to guide and comfort us, and give thyself in the Holy Eucharist to feed and nourish our hungry souls with that sacramental food.

Still thou art really present to us in that holy mystery of love; hence we offer up our devotions in it with our utmost reverence, wonder, and love.

These saving mysteries keep alive our dear Redeemer's death and apply to our souls all the merits of his passion.

These fill our hearts with heroic courage, to do and suffer for the name of Jesus.

These are the food of faith, hope, and love, which fit us for eternal happiness.

O blessed memorial of my Saviour's love and faithful seal of all his promises!

THEE will I bless for all thy mercies; to thee will I open all my necessities.

Begging thy pardon for my past offenses and thy gracious assistance for the time to come.

Imploring the preservation of thy Church and thy blessing upon all the world.

O SPOTLESS LAMB, once slain for us on the cross, and duly commemorated on, and communicated to us at thy holy altar!

Be thou our powerful advocate with thy heavenly Father, and solicit by thy merits his mercy for us.

Offer thyself before his throne, and turn away the wrath we deserve for our sins.

Wherever thou art, we will never forsake thee; and wherever we are, our hearts shall always be with thee.

Friday

Come, let us adore our God that redeemed us.

We wear the badge of a crucified Saviour, and shall we shrink at every cross we meet?

We believe in a God that was crowned with thorns, and shall we abide to tread on nothing but roses?

Before our eyes, O Jesus, we see thee humble and meek, and shall thy servants be proud and insolent?

We see thee travel up and down, poor and unregarded; and shall thy followers strive to be rich and esteemed?

How do we go away from the sacred path which the holy Jesus traced with his own steps!

Pity, O Redeemer, the infirmities of thy children; strengthen with thy grace our fainting hearts.

Arm us, O glorious Conqueror of sin and death, against all the fears and terrors of the world.

Arm all our powers with those celestial virtues of faith, hope, and invincible love,

That we may still go on and resolutely meet whatever stands in our way to heaven.

O GOD, who by our great Master's example hast taught us what labors and sufferings heaven deserves, and that we are to take it by force; confound in us, we beseech thee, the nice tenderness of our nature which is averse to that discipline and hardship we ought to endure as disciples and soldiers of Jesus Christ; help us in our way thither by self-denial and mortification, for the sake of our Lord Jesus Christ, who liveth and reigneth with thee and thy Holy Spirit, ever one God, world without end.

O blessed Jesus, whose grace alone begins and ends and perfects all our hopes!

GRANT, we beseech thee, that by observing diligently thy holy discipline, proposed to us in thy laws, we may correct our levities, and revenge our excesses, and subdue our irregular appetites, and frustrate the temptations of the enemy, and secure our perseverance, and daily proceed to new degrees of virtue and devotion, till in the end of our lives we receive the end of our labors, the salvation of our souls, through our Lord Jesus Christ.

O blessed and all-redeeming Blood, which flowed so freely from the source of life;

Bathe our polluted souls in thy clear streams and purge away all our foul iniquities.

Cleanse us, O merciful Lord, from our secret faults and from those sins that most abuse us.

Wash off the stains our malice has caused in others and those which our weakness has received of them.

Let them not perish by our occasions nor us be undone by theirs.

But let our charity assist one another and thy clemency pardon us all.

Pardon, O gracious Jesus, what we have been; with thy holy discipline correct what we are.

Order by thy providence what we shall be, and in the end crown thine own gifts.

GRANT, we humbly beseech thee, that no experience of good or evil which this day has afforded may be lost on us, but whatever of moment has happened to ourselves or others may render us more skillful in discerning the true value and use of this estate in all the scenes of life, and ready to resign (with our Saviour) our whole concerns and beings here to thy will and the sole advancement of thy glory.

Saturday

GOVERN us with thy grace, O eternal Wisdom, and direct our steps in thy way.

STRENGTHEN us, O Lord, to persevere with courage, that we may never be wanting in our fidelity to thee.

Convince us, blessed Jesus, into this firm judgment, and make our memories faithfully retain it:

Whatever our senses say to deceive us or the world to obscure so beauteous a truth,

That thyself alone art our chief good and the sight of thy glory our supreme felicity.

O GOD, who seest and pitiest the infirmity of our nature, surrounded on every side with dangers and temptations; strengthen us, we beseech thee, with thy all-powerful grace to stand continually on our guard, resolved even to death either warily to avoid or stoutly break through all that offers to divert or stop the advancement of thy love in our hearts; and grant us so wisely to improve the talents of capacity and means thy providence assigns us in this present life that at the great day of account we may every one be received with those precious words: "Well done, thou good and faithful servant: ... enter thou into the joy of thy lord."

Never again, O Jesus, shall those blessed eyes weep, nor thy holy soul be sorrowful to death;

But thou shalt live and reign forever and all created nature perpetually adore thee.

Look up, my soul, and see thy crucified Lord sit gloriously enthroned at the right hand of his Father.

Behold the ragged purple now turned into a robe of light and the scornful reed into a royal scepter.

The wreath of thorns is grown into a sparkling diadem and all his scars polished into brightness.

Live, glorious King of men and angels; live, happy Conqueror of sin and death.

Through fiercest dangers our faith shall follow thee and nothing wrest from us our hope at last to see thee.

May our chief delight be to think of thee and all our study to grow great in thy love.

TEACH us, O Lord, to use this transitory life as pilgrims returning to their beloved home,

That we may take what our journey requires and not think of settling in a foreign country.

O GOD, whose eternal providence has embarked our souls in the ship of our bodies, not to expect any port of anchorage on the sea of this world, but to steer directly through it to thy glorious kingdom; preserve us from the dangers that on all sides assault us, and keep our affections still fitly disposed to receive thy holy inspirations, that being carried strongly forward by thy Holy Spirit we may happily arrive at last in the haven of eternal salvation, through our Lord Jesus Christ.

DEVOTIONS *for* SPECIAL OCCASIONS

THE OFFICE *of* OUR BLESSED SAVIOUR

COME let us ascend to the house of our Lord, where he is truly worshiped and celebrated this day with a holy joy, imploring his mercies for all we need and blessing his bounty for all we have.

So rule us here that we may obey thy grace; so favor us hereafter that we may enjoy thy glory.

LET us not live, O Lord, but to love thee, nor breathe but to speak thy praise, nor be at all but to be all thine.

Blessed be thy holy name, O glorious Son of God, and blessed be thy mercy forever. Thou hast perfectly fulfilled all thy prophets foretold and infinitely transcended all the wonders they admired. Thou hast done enough to convince us into faith and suffered abundantly to inflame us with thy love.

MOST GRACIOUS LORD, who hast so loved the world that thou gavest thyself to redeem it, and humbly tookest upon thee our nature that thou mightest suffer as man for the sins of men and in it familiarly teach us the truth of our salvation; and mightest invincibly also fortify us against all persecutions, and efficaciously draw us after thee into thine own kingdom, by thy holy life and precious death and glorious resurrection: do thou fill our souls with a sense of this wonderful love, that we may live in thy obedience, die in thy favor, and rise again to rejoice with thee forever in thy glory; who, with the Father and the Holy Ghost, livest and reignest, God and King, world without end.

O HOLY and ever-blessed Jesus, who, being the eternal Son of God and most high in the glory of God the Father, didst vouchsafe for us sinners to be born of a humble virgin and suffer intolerable persecutions, even to death upon the cross; work in us, we beseech thee, a due sense of thy infinite love, that adoring and believing in thee as our Lord and Saviour, we may trust in thy infinite merits, imitate thy holy example, obey thy commands, and finally enjoy thy promises, living and reigning with thee, who, with the Father and the Holy Ghost, livest and reignest, God-blessed forever, world without end.

O THOU, my adored Redeemer, be thou the wish of my heart, the scope and end of all my time.

Soon as I awake, let me look up to thee; and when I arise, first lowly bow to thee.

Often in the day let me call in my thoughts to thee; and when I go to rest, close up mine eyes in thee.

So shall my time be governed by thy grace and my eternity crowned with thy glory.

Now our Lord Jesus Christ himself and God even our Father, who hath loved us and given us everlasting salvation and good hope through grace, comfort our hearts and stablish us in every good word and work.

THE OFFICE of the HOLY GHOST

Kindle in our hearts, O Lord, thy holy fire, that we may offer to thee the incense of praise.

IF in the Church there be any wisdom or knowledge, if any real sanctity or decent order,

If any faith in the mysteries of religion, if any hope of everlasting salvation,

If any love of God as our sovereign bliss, if any charity one toward another,

All flows from thee and thy free grace, O thou boundless Ocean of eternal mercies!

All flows from thee, and may we all return our little streams in tribute to thy bounty.

Let us remember, our God is a pure Spirit and delights to dwell in a calm tabernacle.

CURE us, O thou great Physician of souls, of all our sinful distempers.

Cure us of this intermitting piety, and fix it into an even and a constant holiness.

Oh, make us use religion as our regular diet and not only as a medicine in necessity.

Make us enter into a course of hearty repentance and practice virtue as our daily exercise.

So shall our souls be endued with perfect health and disposed for a long, even for an everlasting, life.

LET not our faith grow wild with superfluous branches, nor be stripped into a naked and fruitless trunk.

Let not our hope swell up to rash presumption, nor shrink away into a faint despair.

Let not our love be cooled into a careless indifferency nor heated into a furious zeal.

Suffer us not obstinately to persist in any known wickedness, nor maliciously to impugn any known truth.

Suffer us not to die in our sins without repentance, but have mercy upon us at that serious hour, and inspire us with thy grace now and always.

O GOD, who by thy Holy Spirit didst at first establish a Church, and who, sanctifying it by the same Spirit, dost still preserve and govern it; hear, we beseech thee, the prayers of thy servants, and mercifully grant us the perpetual assistance of thy grace, that we may never be deceived by any false spirit, nor overcome by the suggestions of flesh and blood, but in all our doubts may be directed in the ways of truth and in all our actions guided by this thy Holy Spirit; who, with thee and thy eternal Son, liveth and reigneth, one God, world without end.

O ALMIGHTY GOD, and Father of all mercies, who alone canst order the unruly wills and affections of sinful men, and who didst in the beginning powerfully instruct and graciously lead thy faithful servants by sending them the light of thy Holy Spirit; grant us by the same Spirit to have a right judgment in all things that are necessary to our salvation, and refusing the comforts and pleasures of this world, continually to rejoice in his holy consolation. Give us, we beseech thee, the spirit of wisdom and understanding and counsel, that by the inspiration thereof we may think those things that are good; the spirit of faith and fortitude and power, that by the guidance thereof we may perform the same in a manner most acceptable to thee; and give us the spirit of prayer and supplication, that we may adore thee in spirit, with reverence, steadfastness, and perseverance. Through Jesus Christ, our Lord.

THE OFFICE of the SAINTS

Come, let us adore the King of Saints.

They who now are gladly arrived at the quiet harbor of eternal rest,

They beheld us here below embarked in the same ship and bound with all our interests for the same port.

They beheld us struggling yet in this sea of storms, while they are safely landed on the coasts of everlasting light and joy.

Thou art ready to guide us safely through all our dangers, even as thou hast guided them.

Let the heavens therefore hear thy voice, and let all the powers thereof give glory unto thee.

Command now thy angels to watch about us and carry us to the place of our desires.

O praise the Lord, all ye powers of my soul, praise the immortal King of saints and angels.

Praise him in the mighty hosts of angels, whom he sets about us as the guard of our lives;

That they may safely keep us in all our ways and carry us at last to their own home.

Blessed forever be the eternal Spirit, whose grace brings all the saints to glory.

God and his holy angels are on our side, Jesus takes our part, and his blessed saints rejoice over us.

O GOD, whose merciful providence has still from the beginning sown the seeds of grace in the hearts of thy chosen servants, which at the resurrection of thy Son (the first fruits of them that sleep) sprang up into glory, who, by his holy doctrine and life and precious death, hast infinitely increased the means of salvation and the number of thy saints; grant, we beseech thee, that we, whom thou hast favored with so many advantages by calling us into communion with them may obtain thy grace to imitate them here and to rejoice with them in thy kingdom hereafter, through the same our Lord Jesus Christ, their and our merciful Redeemer; to whom, with thee and the Holy Ghost, be all glory forever.

THE OFFICE *for a* FAMILY

Morning

In the name of the Father and of the Son and of the Holy Ghost. Amen.

O GOD THE FATHER, Creator of the world, have mercy upon us.

O God the Son, Redeemer of mankind, have mercy upon us.

O God the Holy Ghost, Perfecter of the faithful, have mercy upon us.

Holy, holy, holy, Lord God of hosts!

Have mercy on this family, we beseech thee;

And spare every soul therein for thy name's sake.

Come, let us adore the dayspring from on high.

O GLORIOUS JESUS, without whom we are dead; quicken us with thy Spirit that we may live by thy life; and so putting thee on, may make no more provision for the flesh to fulfill its desires; but for the spirit only, thereby to fulfill all righteousness in thee and bring forth the fruits of the Holy Ghost; while by thy power we cast away the works of darkness and put on the impregnable armor of light.

ALMIGHTY GOD and most merciful Father, give us, we beseech thee, that grace that we may duly examine the inmost of our hearts and our most secret thoughts, how we stand before thee; and that we may henceforth never be drawn to do anything that may dishonor thy name, but may persevere in all good purposes and in thy holy service unto our lives' end: and grant that we may this day begin to walk before thee as those that are called to an inheritance of light in Christ.

O LORD, we give thee humble and hearty thanks for all the benefits and blessings, both spiritual and temporal, which in the riches of thy great mercy thou hast bountifully poured down upon us. Let us not live but to praise and magnify thy glorious name. Particularly we give thee most unfeigned thanks for our preservation from the time of our birth to this present, for bringing us safe to the beginning of this day, in which and all the days of our life, we beseech thee, preserve us from sin and from danger, so governing and leading us that all our thoughts, words, and works may tend to the honor and glory of thy name, the good of thy Church, the discharge of our duties, and the salvation of our souls, through Jesus Christ, our only Saviour and Redeemer.

O ETERNAL GOD and merciful Father, we humbly beseech thee, bless thy holy Church wheresoever spread upon the whole earth. Purge it from all heresy, schism, superstition, and factious maintenance of groundless opinions; that one faith, one Lord, one baptism, may in all places be uniformly professed, as thy Church is and can be but one. And grant that we here present may be, and continue, faithful, living, and working members under Christ the head in that Church the body all the days of our lives and through the hour of our death, for the merits and by the grace of the same Jesus Christ, our Lord and only Saviour.

O MERCIFUL GOD, bless this particular church in which we live. Make it, and all the members of it, sound in faith and holy in life; but especially so illumine all its ministers with the true knowledge of Christ and understanding of thy word, according as thy Spirit meant it, that both by their preaching and living, they may set it forth to thy glory, and that all thy people committed to their charge may from their mouths meekly hear thy word, receive it with pure affection, and through thy gracious assistance bring forth the fruits of the Spirit, for the honor of Jesus Christ, our mediator and advocate.

Evening

Day by day we will speak of the glory of thy empire, and night after night will we utter the memory of thy great goodness and of thy tender mercies that are over all thy works.

SAVE us, good Lord, waking, and keep us sleeping; that we may watch with Christ and rest in peace.

As is thy majesty, so is thy mercy, O gracious Father; and therefore we beseech thee to hear our humble supplication for the forgiveness of our sins. Forgive them all, O Lord, of what kind or degree soever they be:

our sins of omission and our sins of commission;

the sins of our youth and the sins of our riper years;

the sins of our souls and the sins of our bodies;

our secret and our more open sins;

our sins of ignorance and surprise, and our more deliberate and presumptuous sins;

the sins we have done to please ourselves and the sins we have done to please others;

the sins we know and remember, and the sins we have forgotten;

the sins we have striven to hide from others and the sins by which we have made others offend;

forgive them, O Lord, forgive them all for his sake who died for our sins and rose again for our justification, and now stands at thy right hand to make intercession for us, Jesus Christ our Lord.

O GOD, the only rest of our wearied souls, the only joy of our time and of our eternity;

Have mercy upon us.

From all manner of evil, but especially from sin; from all occasions of offending thy divine Majesty and from the particular temptations to which by time, place, or temper we are most exposed;

Deliver us, O Lord.

From the treachery of our own hearts and the violence of our passions;

Deliver us, O Lord.

By thy almighty power and unsearchable wisdom; by thy adorable goodness and all thy other glorious attributes;

Deliver us, O Lord.

By the mystery of thy holy incarnation and humble birth; by the sanctity of thy heavenly doctrine, the perfect example of thy heavenly life; and by all the miracles thou didst work for us;

Deliver us, O Lord.

By the merits of thy bitter passion and death; by thy victorious resurrection; by thy triumphant ascension and by the glory of thy kindom, who art King of kings and Lord of lords, in the hour of death and in the day of judgment;

Deliver us, O Lord

We sinners beseech thee to hear us, O Lord God; and that it may please thee to give us true repentance for all our past offenses and to work in us a firm and effectual resolution to amend our lives for the time to come;

We beseech thee to hear us, O Lord.

That it may please thee to pardon the sins of our life and so to prevent and assist us with thy grace while we live here, that we may not fail to be eternally happy hereafter;

We beseech thee to hear us, O Lord.

That it may please thee to have pity on the infirmities

of our frail nature and in all our dangers, trials, and temptations to strengthen and relieve us;

> *We beseech thee to hear us, O Lord.*

That we may live in peace and charity with all the world, especially among ourselves, united into one family, patiently forbearing, freely forgiving, and readily assisting one another;

> *We beseech thee to hear us, O Lord.*

That in the midst of our daily business we may lift up our hearts to heaven and thereby comfort and refresh our spirits;

> *We beseech thee to hear us, O Lord.*

That whether we sleep or wake, we may be safe under thy protection, who never slumberest nor sleepest; and whether we live or die, we may always be thine;

> *We beseech thee to hear us, O Lord.*

ACCEPT, O gracious Father, this our evening sacrifice of most humble and hearty thanks for all the mercies and blessings of this day, and not only of this day, but of all the days of our past lives.

KEEP us in safety under the shadow of thy wings, for unto thy almighty protection we commit ourselves this night, humbly beseeching thee that after due rest we may rise with thankful hearts and return with cheerful dispositions to the duties of our several vocations, to glorify thee by our good works, through Jesus Christ our Lord.

God, the Father of our Lord Jesus Christ, the God of the patriarchs and prophets, the God of the apostles, martyrs, and confessors, and of all true believers; increase our faith, confirm our hope, and enlarge our charity; and grant that we may faithfully serve him by doing and suffering his will all the days of our short pilgrimage here and after death be made partakers of immortal glory.

THE OFFICE for a TROUBLED SPIRIT

O most blessed and gracious God, who only canst heal a wounded spirit and quiet a troubled mind; unto thee do I cry for help.

O thou great Physician of body and soul, uphold and comfort my weak and dejected spirit. As thou alone canst relieve me, so unto thee do I call for relief. Oh, hear my most earnest supplication and make me to possess an easy, quiet, and cheerful spirit, as my trust is in thee.

It is good that thou both hope and quietly wait for the salvation of the Lord.

Return unto thy rest, O my soul; and be no longer disquieted within me.

Return unto thy rest, O my soul, in God; for he is thy resting place and thy salvation.

INDEX